SPLIT SECOND CHOICE

CHOICE

The Power of Attitude

Additional Praise for Split Second Choice

Halliburton Energy Services
"A well-used tool we utilize to drive us to success implementing new systems and processes in our business."
- Larry Lemarie, Sales Manager

Picadilly Cafeterias
"It hits the responsible party right between the eyes."
- Ronnie LaBorde, President

Dyntek
"Helps our people excel in the relationships that drive our highly technical business."
- Alan Reed, Regional Vice President

Gulf South Business Systems & Consultants, Inc.
"Jim...I read your book, meditated on its ideas, reread those ideas, and now keep it handy to refer to like a "handy" mentor to remind me to "recommit."
- Robert Shreve, Chairman/CEO

Workshop Participants
"You've been reading my mail."
"You were looking right into my mind."
"Wow, this works in all aspects of my life."

SPLIT SECOND CHOICE

The Power of Attitude

By James L. Winner
with George P. Thompson III

THE WINNERS • LOUISIANA

The Winners LLC
Baton Rouge, LA

First Edition
Copyright © 1996 by James L. Winner
and George P. Thompson III
Third Edition
Copyright © 2013 by James L. Winner
and George P. Thompson III

Third Edition
Abridged From First Edition
With Additional Material

Printed and bound in the United States of
America.

Cover Graphic by Andy & Emily Thompson

ISBN 978-0-9892103-0-0

IN LOVING MEMORY

While growing up, I watched my parents constantly rise above the obstacles in their lives. They taught me that when you get knocked down, you just get back up. This book is dedicated to the memory of my parents, Lowell and Louise Winner.

My father had only a ninth grade education, but he didn't let that stop him. His desire to win was tremendous. By age 28, he owned the farm in Michigan where I started my life.

In the late 1940's, he sold the farm and bought some property on a highway to build the restaurant of his dreams. Things went well until the highway began changing into an interstate. The chaos of the new road construction reduced traffic flow and forced my parents into bankruptcy.

Almost immediately, they were back on their feet attitudinally. With very little money, they moved our family of six to Albuquerque, New Mexico to start over.

The day after we arrived, I remember my Dad walking to Highway 66 full of enthusiasm. He continued walking for seven miles toward the center of town until he secured a job at a service station. My mother was able to get a job at a laundry nearby, and all of us kids did what we could to help. By pooling our resources we were able to pay the rent on a very small house. We had no furniture. We slept in our sleeping bags, and cooked on a Coleman stove. The back bedroom where my brother Lee and I slept was cold enough to be used as a refrigerator, and it worked quite well.

Those were tough times for my family, but we shared love and closeness and concern for each other. Even though we were very poor financially, we simply were not poor in spirit because of my parents. As time went on, things improved dramatically.

Many years later, hard times struck again when my dad lost his job. After 17 years with American Car and Foundry, he was laid off. When he realized that his whole future was in jeopardy, he picked up an Alaskan magazine, and out of the clear blue he said, "I'm going to Alaska." Through some contacts my brother had, Dad began talking to someone about taking a job driving a garbage truck. Most people would not even consider working as a garbage truck driver, but my dad never saw it as anything but an opportunity.

My mother tolerated his absence for a few months, then told me to get the truck ready. That meant she was planning to drive a 1965 Dodge crew cab with five-speed standard transmission, no power brakes and no power steering, from New Mexico to Alaska to be with my father.

She called to tell him she was coming. When he told her not to come, she hung up on him because she had already closed out her retirement account and packed the truck. She was determined to go. Moments later, the phone rang, with my father on the line. I only heard my mother's side of the conversation, but she said, "Well, I just want you to understand that nothing in my life is more important to me than you. If I have to sleep on the floor, I will, but I'm coming."

I watched her take that Dodge crew cab with all of her belongings and head down the highway. Because she was only four feet, nine inches tall, she had to sit on a pillow to see through the windshield. She drove that truck through all of the Canadian Rockies, and on to Alaska.

My father worked on the garbage truck for about 90 days before he became manager of the officer's club at Clear Air Force Base. Then he homesteaded, and opened up a snow machine dealership and a Buck knife franchise. Eventually, he and my mother moved to Valdez, where they bought another home and worked until retirement.

No matter what happened, they always kept their dreams in focus, maintained their committment, and moved forward with unquenchable enthusiasm. They lived the concept outlined in this book, and that is why they are such a great inspiration to me.

Thank you Lord for lifting us up when we were weary. We know without you this book would not be a reality.
To God Be the Glory!

But those who wait on the LORD shall renew their strength; they shall mount up with wings like eagles, they shall run and not be weary, they shall walk and not faint.
Isaiah 40:31

ACKNOWLEDGMENTS

I have wanted to publish this book for a very long time. Over twenty years ago, my associate George Thompson said, "Jim, if you really want to write that book, I have a pretty good understanding of computers and how to structure a book, and you have a wonderful grasp of the concept. If you will just audio tape what you think ought to be in it, I'll pull it all together."

In retrospect, I don't think either one of us had any idea what would be involved in writing a book, but this one would not exist without George's total commitment. Working in and around all of his family responsibilities until it was finished, he succeeded where many others have failed. He, in turn, credits his wife, Kathy, for her unwavering support, and the many hours she spent helping him get the words just right.

I would also like to thank my wife, Margaret, for her support. Eight years ago I showed her an early manuscript I put together on my own, and she said, "Sounds great. Let's print it!" Through each draft, she has remained dedicated to her conviction that this concept should be in the hands of thousands of readers where it can impact their lives in a positive and healthy way. So again, thank you Margaret.

As anyone who has ever published a book knows, there are many people assisting at various points along the way. Although there are far too many to name individually, I would particularly like to thank Mike Martin, Bob Sabino, Gary Suboter, and Jean Hamrick for their precious gifts of time, guidance, wisdom, and encouragement.

Contents

FOREWORD

Our world is changing rapidly. Individuals and companies are struggling to get ahead and stay ahead. People are grappling with adversity on all fronts. Positions that were once secure are no longer secure. Companies are fighting to stay in business. There is much downsizing, restructuring and trauma. And it is a safe bet that the future will continue to challenge us.

This quite naturally leads to the question, "How can we cope with the changes?" Or, better yet, "How can we gain an advantage?"

As many have already discovered, a fundamental component of success is the right attitude. We cannot be customer driven until we are customer focused attitudinally. We cannot produce quality work for our customers unless we are excited about doing so. We cannot attract and retain quality employees without the right attitude towards commitment. We cannot sustain innovation and continual improvement unless we know how to recommit continuously to the challenges of change.

Attitude is critical to success!

Attitude is frequently regarded as an issue that each person must confront individually, yet it is *not* just an individual issue. Groups and teams have attitudes. Corporations have attitudes. And while leadership is an important component in the search for a positive, progressive attitude, evidence suggests that individuals hold the key to a group or company attitude, because the attitude of these organizations is the sum total of the attitudes of its individuals. Because individuals are in control of the group's attitude, they hold the key to success in the quality movement and to organizational success, as well.

Attitude also makes the difference between success — which in today's world means "getting by" — and winning.

Pat Riley, the well-known head coach of the Los Angeles Lakers basketball team, was quoted in a story in *Personal Selling Power Magazine* as follows:

> "The difference between success and winning is in a person's attitude. When I speak before a business audience or talk to my team, I don't talk about success, failure or winning and losing because I don't want to paint that kind of picture. I've always believed that anybody can be successful. If you're a competitive person, and you're striving or aspiring to be the best, then really it's about being that one winner who will somehow find a way to shoot up out of the pack of everybody else who's successful.
>
> "I've found that the people who apply themselves, learn the proper techniques, understand the philosophies, plans, systems and strategies of their organization, take pride in the work and repeat it every single day, are the people who will become skillful and maximize whatever talents they originally brought to the job. The difference between people who are skillful and merely successful, and the ones who win is in attitude. The attitude a person develops is the most important ingredient in determining the level of success."[1]

Throughout history, learned individuals and scholars have shared Pat Riley's viewpoint. William James, known as the father of modern psychology, once wrote that the greatest discovery of his generation was how human beings could alter their lives by altering their attitudes of mind. This is such a profound statement, yet most of us pass through life without ever grasping its significance. Sadder still, very few of us ever learn how to harness our attitude power, even when we recognize it.

Many other authors have written about how attitude makes the difference and about why your attitude should be positive. We totally agree with the philosophy presented in these books, but like many good things in life, they leave us wanting more. They admonish us to have a positive attitude, giving us example after example of how positive attitudes make things happen and how negative attitudes lead to poor results. They teach us to be aware of our attitudes and even give us a few suggestions for improving them. Sadly, however, they leave us on our own for the most difficult part, which is recognizing the point when our attitude is shifting from positive to negative. In other words, they don't really tell us how to control our attitude.

How *do* you control your attitude? How do you recognize when attitude is a roadblock on your highway? The answers are fairly simple but not widely recognized.

We know that much of life follows a pattern because there are patterns in our daily behavior, patterns in our growth and development and even patterns in our grieving process.[2] As we will discover in this book, there is also a pattern to our attitude. This pattern leads us to make instinctive choices. While these choices are frequently good, they can just as easily be destructive. The good news is that we can choose to control our attitude for any desired level of success in life.

This book is dedicated to helping you, the reader, reach an understanding of the attitude cycles that individuals and organizations experience. It will help you see attitude roadblocks and help direct you around them. You will learn about a split-second choice: what choice to make, why it is important and when and how to make it. You will also learn about turning negative situations into positive ones and how to sustain the fundamental attitude pattern necessary for ongoing success.

I am confident that this book will make a positive difference in your life.

PREFACE TO THE THIRD EDITION

Many books have been written on the subject of attitude, perhaps because there is universal agreement that attitude is a critical building block for success.

Since this book was originally published in 1996, thousands of people have been introduced to the concept of what we have designated as a "Split Second Choice." And the feedback we receive is universally the same.... "You've been reading my mail," they say. Then they add that someone in their circle needs to read this, or that their organization needs to understand it and apply it. We are glad the earlier editions of this book have had such a positive impact on so many people, and we're pleased to be able to offer this third, even stronger edition.

It is a timeless concept, and certainly one of the most valuable tools you will ever encounter. Like certain laws of the universe, the principles in this book are simply foundational. Without them, it is difficult to reach the higher levels of success.

We have listened to the feedback of many readers, and have revised this edition to produce even better results for those who will scour its pages with their eyes, devour the pearls of wisdom, and apply the simple lessons within.

Although this concept applies to everyone and virtually every situation, it seems to resonate in a particularly powerful way with leaders and salespeople. Perhaps this is because sales is a profession where you simply cannot find significant and repeatable success unless you can control your attitude. And it's common knowledge that leaders are faced with "attitude problems" on a daily basis. Both of these groups will find comfort in these pages.

In this edition we have added a specific new chapter for those of you in any kind of sales and/or marketing business –

particularly those where you profit by recruiting people to join your team – but actually, any business where rejection is frequent. Careers like these offer virtually unlimited potential, yet somehow success still eludes some of those who demonstrate the necessary courage to begin. This new chapter was written to help more people – perhaps including you – succeed in that type of career. And although this chapter was added with that primary purpose in mind, it will benefit anyone who wants to thoroughly understand their attitude and be in a position to control it for the better.

As we begin, let us congratulate you on your obvious desire to improve your life by better understanding and controlling your attitude.

[1]Gerhard and L.B. Gschwandtner, *Personal Selling Power*, January/February 1991, p. 73

[2]Kubler-Ross, Elizabeth, **On Death and Dying**

Chapter 1

BEGINNINGS

"The longer I live, the more I realize the impact of attitude on life. Attitude, to me, is more important than facts. It is more important than the past, than education, than money, than circumstances, than failures, than successes, than what other people think or say or do. It is more important than appearance, giftedness or skill. It will make or break a company... a church... a home. The remarkable thing is we have a choice every day regarding the attitude we will embrace for that day. We cannot change our past... we cannot change the fact that people will act in a certain way... we cannot change the inevitable. The only thing we can do is play on the one string we have, and that is our attitude. ... I am convinced that life is 10% what happens to me and 90% how I react to it."

From Attitude by Charles Swindoll

Do you ever wonder why some people have unlimited success and happiness in their lives, while others spend much of their time in misery or mediocrity? I do.

As a professional trainer and speaker, I meet a lot of successful individuals. I also work with many people who are not experiencing the success they could. My goal as a trainer is to serve both groups.

Like others before me, I have found that attitude makes the biggest difference in our ability to succeed. During the course of marketing my training programs, I discovered a process that can help us take control of our attitude. This book is about the decision-making process all of us experience along the attitude pathways of life. It will help us make good choices, at the appropriate times.

Several years ago, I went to see one of my training customers. As I walked around his business, it amazed me to find that many of his employees had moved on to jobs with other companies. Because employee turnover is common to all companies, I did not pay much attention to this observation at the time. A couple of months later, I noticed the same phenomenon at another organization. This time, my curiosity got the best of me, and I began to conduct some research with people I knew. I asked questions such as, "Why do people change employers and careers so quickly?" and "Why do they change them so often?" Since turnover is an expensive problem for any business, I knew I could help my clients if I discovered methods to reduce the expense.

As I met with more clients, I continued to observe people changing jobs, and I kept asking questions. I spoke with hundreds of people over the months that followed, and I began hearing repetition in their answers. I knew there must be a pattern to the answers, but it was not clear to me at that point.

A couple of years into my research, I faced problems in my own career. It looked as if a job change might be in order for me, too. To prevent making a decision I might later regret, I decided to compare my own situation to those I had been observing. In a sudden flash of insight, I realized that *our attitude cycles in and out of four major phases during our lives.* With this observation, I quickly pinpointed my own position in the pattern. My career was not the problem. It was my attitude! Armed with this new insight, I quickly fixed my attitude by making the simple choice the pattern suggested. I stayed with the career I already had and advanced from there. My crisis was over.

As I continued to evaluate my findings, I was surprised to find that the *type* of career is seldom a factor when people decide to make a job change. The educational background of the employee is not important, either. Gender, age, location, nationality, race — none of these factors seem to matter. With this improved understanding, I began paying attention to the choices other people were making. Clearly, successful people were making the same choice I had made, and not only in their careers, but in all aspects of their lives. This choice, and the process that surrounds it, is the subject of this book. I believe that making this choice consistently is what allows SUPER ACHIEVERS to accomplish phenomenal results, in spite of inevitable obstacles and setbacks.

Roughly half of this book is devoted to an understanding of how our attitude cycles in and out of these four major phases (and their associated subphases). The rest deals with practical application, both on the job and in other areas of our lives. While this material is extremely useful in difficult situations, including career moves, *it is really a tool for everyday use.* These concepts apply to *all* areas of our lives. They apply to marriage, school, community affairs, church and synagogue, hobbies and projects, everyday living — even politics. They will help parents understand and communicate with their children. They will help supervisors understand and communicate with their team members. They will help husbands and wives understand each other and improve their relationships, and they can help YOU understand and control your own actions.

As part of my training activities, I now present these ideas in a variety of workshop settings. During these encounters, heads nod in agreement as we review the various phases and subphases.

Afterwards, people say to me, "You've been reading my mail." or "You were looking right into my mind." I have found that these concepts hit home for everyone, without exception. The insight they provide is powerful. Indeed, individuals and companies alike have progressed and accelerated after learning these secrets.

Because the workshop format has proven to be so successful for so many, I have chosen to present this material as if you were experiencing your own private workshop. I will be asking you to mentally place yourself in a traditional job setting long enough for me to explain the fundamentals. If you have never held a job, fear not; you will find it easy to follow along. If your chosen profession is raising a family, simply apply these concepts to that occupation. With two toddlers at home and three grown children, I know from personal experience that the job of raising a family is just as challenging as any other.

Before plunging into the workshop, it will be helpful to understand what I mean by a split-second choice.

A long time ago, I was driving a 1966 Corvette to Farmington, New Mexico. The highway was long and lonely, and the sun was going down. I pushed the gas pedal down firmly, releasing 600 mechanical horses under the hood. As the speedometer needle moved forward, I leaned back to relax and let my thoughts drift.

Minutes later, as the car edged over the top of a hill, my reverie snapped. A flock of sheep was standing right in the middle of the highway. I had a split-second decision to make. My options were limited — panic and let fate take its negative course, or take control in a positive way.

Thanks to many years of experience drag racing and driving on dirt tracks, I *automatically* chose the positive approach. I engaged a series of hard braking maneuvers, which sent the car looping and spinning a couple of times. When it finally stopped in a big cloud of dust, my pride was wounded, my brakes were smoking and my cardiovascular system was on full alert. Thankfully, the sheep and I were all alive, and my car was still operative. My split-second decision to act in a positive way had saved us all.

Frequently, when dealing with our careers, our relationships and our daily lives, you and I will find a "flock of sheep" on our attitude highway. The obstacle may not appear as suddenly as the sheep did on my trip to Farmington, but we still have a decision to make. Whether we make a snap decision, or take time to analyze the situation, we experience a split-second point in which the decision is made. As you will soon see, *choosing wisely at those split-second points will strongly influence our success in life. Those split-second choices are crucial.*

This book will help you recognize the critical decision points in your life, career, projects and relationships. It will also help you recognize the habitual decision rule you are using at those critical points. When you can "see" those turning points, the paths they offer and the habitual choice you are making, you can consistently follow the path that is best for you. You can develop a habit that will suit you well.

On my trip to Farmington, I made the right choice, thanks to a well-developed habit. When we make the right attitude choice a habit, it is easier to be a champion for ourselves and for others.

Now get ready, because it's time to begin reading with EXCITEMENT!

SPLIT SECOND CHOICE

Chapter 2

The First Phase: EXCITEMENT

"I never did a day's work in my life. It was all fun."
Thomas Edison

"If you have a dream, you have everything."
Robert Schuller

Let's begin your workshop by setting the scene. Suppose you are a company president, and you have just hired me. Today is my first day on the job.

Over the last few weeks, you and I met for several interviews. During the first interview, you decided *I could do* the job, that *I wanted to do* the job and that *I would fit in* with your organization.

For the second interview, you asked me to bring my wife, Margaret, along. To validate your initial feelings about me, you had us talk with several other people in your company. They all agreed with your conclusion that I would be *perfect* for the job and that Margaret and I were an excellent team.

With this agreement, the stage was set for you and me to meet again. In this third meeting, we discussed what you wanted me to accomplish in my new position. You talked about how I was the ideal candidate to achieve great things. Together, we talked about goals and how they would be attained: You painted a picture of my job responsibilities and career opportunities, and I painted a picture of my abilities and commitment. When those two pictures snapped together like the pieces of a jigsaw puzzle, we made the decision to team up. You offered me the job, and I accepted. Then we embellished the picture with images of victory, rewards and glory.

EXCITEMENT PHASE
Dream
Initial Commitment

My future appeared brighter than ever. Beaming with a feeling of euphoria, I went home and told Margaret, "This job is *exactly* what I want. It's the perfect opportunity for me." I also hastened to explain to anyone else who would listen that I was embarking on a magnificent new career, one filled with great promise.

So here I am, feeling like a surfer who just caught the big wave ... a thousand fans on the beach ... the sun bright ... the water bluer than blue ... the beaches whiter than white. With this on-top-of-the-world feeling and dreams of even better things ahead, I have started my new career with you. These dreams of the future sparkle, and they energize all of my activities. There is an energy inside me that is focused on projects and results. I antici-pate nothing but good things. I am really EXCITED about the opportunity before me.

As I start this first day, I also feel committed to the job. I'm not sure how long my commitment will last, and neither are you, but we both perceive it's deep enough to cultivate a win-win relationship.

My engine is revved up, and I'm ready to roll. I can already see the checkered flag waving me on to a victory lap. Because I am truly EXCITED, and because my commitment level is high, any obstacle or complication in the early days of my new career will be easy to handle. I will either leap over, walk around, duck under or just break straight through the difficulty. If things don't happen exactly the way I want them to, I will shrug it off and move on. My attitudinal pendulum is tilted full positive, in a sort of full-speed-ahead position. My enthusiasm level is high, and I am generally very productive.

EXCITEMENT

FULL TILT POSITIVE

You may be asking yourself, "Does it really happen this way?" Of course it does. Maybe not always at the level described here, but every time we start a new career, project or relationship, we begin with a positive attitude. Since this phase of our attitude cycle is often accompanied by emotion, enthusiasm and energetic behavior, I have labelled it EXCITEMENT. We have a dream in mind, and we make a commitment to the career, project or relationship. *All of these feelings and dreams are very real,* and for a while, everything seems to go our way.

Unfortunately, it is difficult for us to keep our ***dreams*** in clear focus for the long time periods encompassed by careers, projects and relationships. Maintaining a high level of ***commitment*** over the long term is equally challenging. The hundreds of people I interviewed told me they can usually sustain commitment for 90 days or so, but after six months, it becomes very difficult. So, unless I am a rare exception, my attitude of EXCITEMENT towards my new job with you will last just three to six months. Then it will begin to diminish. And a second phase will strike.

SPLIT SECOND CHOICE

Chapter 3

The Second Phase: FRUSTRATION

"People may fail many times, but they become failures only when they begin to blame someone else."

Anonymous

"If you find a path with no obstacles, it probably doesn't lead anywhere."

Frank Clark

Let's continue the discussion about my job with you. It is now three to six months after I started. The energy of my initial EXCITEMENT is beginning to wear off, and I am beginning to experience more of the realities of my job. It is much more difficult than I anticipated. There are so many things I want to do, and I want to do them well, but things just aren't going the way I expected. I probably don't even realize it, but I'm beginning to shift into a second attitudinal phase. I have labelled this phase FRUSTRATION because of the feelings involved.

For any long-term commitment, and for many short-term commitments, as well, a FRUSTRATION phase follows the

EXCITEMENT phase like night follows day. It's inevitable.

To see how frustration enters our lives, lay this book down for a moment and try this experiment. First, clasp your hands together by intertwining your fingers. Then look down at your hands. Which thumb is on top? The right one or the left? Now, reverse your hands so that the other thumb is on top. Be sure and reverse all of your fingers, too. This second position is very uncomfortable because all of your life, you've been in the habit of putting your hands together a certain way.

If you decide to change that habit (and, by the way, there's no compelling reason to do that, because whether you are left or right thumbed makes no difference), it will require a period of discomfort while you practice the new habit. During that practice period, you have to accept the discomfort. That's what happens in the start-up phase of a new career.

Discomfort is attached to the new habits and skills we are developing. It's a perfectly natural part of the learning process, and it's okay to feel frustrated, especially when we take on new challenges.

IF YOU ARE UNWILLING TO BEAR DISCOMFORT, YOU WILL NOT MAKE PROGRESS TOWARD A DIFFICULT GOAL! YOU MUST COMMIT YOURSELF AND PREPARE TO ACCEPT THE FRUSTRATION.

Back to my career with you: The FRUSTRATION I'm experiencing injects a cloud of confusion into my mind. I feel like a juggler who has picked up one pin too many, and I'm struggling to keep everything moving smoothly. Doubt arrives on the scene, and I find myself asking, "Was it the right decision to come to work for you?" Because of the doubt, my enthusiasm begins to drop. Anxiety comes into play, and my productivity may fall, too.

As my boss, you may not even notice my attitude beginning to slip. If you do, you'll probably just chalk it up to the stress of the job or assume I've got a problem at home. But it begins to dawn on me, vividly, that, "Hey, I'm in trouble." How can this be happening? This was the perfect opportunity for me. You thought so, and so did I.

I'M IN MY FRUSTRATION PHASE!

Let's back up for a moment and examine what just happened in more detail.

I started out EXCITED about my new job with you, and now it's a few months later. The EXCITEMENT phase is beginning to wear off and is being replaced by a FRUSTRATION phase. As you will see, this FRUSTRATION phase can have either four or six subphases, depending on the path we choose to take. But regardless of the path, it starts out with the same four subphases.

1. SHOCK

The first subphase of my frustration experience is SHOCK. I am shocked at the reality of just how *challenging* this job really is, thinking to myself, "Impossible. No way. Just couldn't be this difficult." In this subphase, my attitude pendulum begins to drop away from full positive.

SHOCK

MOMENTUM SHIFTS

2. DENIAL

The next subphase is DENIAL. I react defensively to the shock and deny responsibility for many aspects of my commitment to you. It's human nature to do this. I will not admit that I understood *from the beginning* how difficult the job would be. I might even catch myself saying, "Listen, I checked this out carefully, so I can't be responsible for the way I'm feeling." In this subphase, my pendulum is still on the positive side, but it's changing position fast, and my enthusiasm is really beginning to wane. I have given up control of my attitude by denying responsibility for my situation.

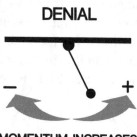

DENIAL

MOMENTUM INCREASES

3. FEAR

As the frustration continues, and I continue to deny responsibility for my problem, I move into FEAR. I become fearful that I've been trapped and that I won't be able to escape. I start saying to myself, "I expected *some* difficulties, but not all this!"

FEAR

WHICH WAY?

Questions begin to enter my mind, like, "Am I competent? Will I be discovered? What will others think? Did I made a mistake coming to work here? Am I trapped? Is this career what I thought it would be? What will happen if these problems never clear up? Will I ever be okay again?"

What if ... what if ... what if ...?

The resulting fear further inhibits my performance, and my attitude slides into neutral — neither positive nor negative. My focus is diffused and muddled. My commitment drops considerably, and my enthusiasm lacks positive direction. I'm probably not going to cause the company any damage at this point, but it's unlikely that I'll do many positive things, either. Making matters worse, the momentum built up by the natural swing of the pendulum now has my attitude *accelerating towards negative.*

If you leave me in this FEAR subphase for an extended period of time, what emotion will eventually erupt? You're right! I'll become defensive and ANGRY!

4. ANGER

My fears lead to ANGER. In one of man's most natural responses, my systems react defensively, seeking to protect me. I start out angry because *of the way I feel,* and then I look for other targets, like you!

ANGER

INNER OR OUTER-DIRECTED?

The ANGER subphase is a precarious position for me — a pivotal point. It is where I make a split-second decision, usually out of habit. As noted above, my attitude leaving the FEAR subphase is neutral, but my overall shifting momentum has me headed in the negative direction. Will I continue in a negative direction or stop it and swing back to positive? We'll take up the positive direction in a later chapter. But for now, let's assume momentum carries me to a negative reaction as it frequently seems to do.

NEGATIVE CYCLE

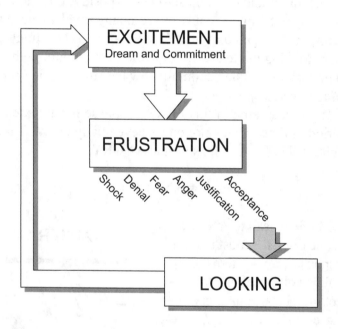

I have just chosen a negative attitude cycle. This decision to "go with the flow" causes me to lash out with negative, outward-directed anger. With outward-directed anger, everyone and everything else is the cause of my frustration — everyone, that is, except me.

The Chinese say, "Four horses cannot overtake the tongue," and that will apply to me. My tongue starts wagging, and I pass out complaints and anger to anyone who will listen:

spouse, parents, family, and friends. If there are some generally negative people around, I'll probably start hanging out with them. We'll gravitate towards each other because they will be quick to agree with what I have to say. This will simply reinforce my anger.

Helpful, supportive people — who might understand the frustrations I'm feeling and be in a position to help — may begin backing away from me. I might even push them away without meaning to. As a friend of mine, you might try to help by saying, "Jim, you've got an attitude problem." There's a good chance I would explode and say, "Back off! It's none of your business!"

This anger is born of a type of fear that makes people incredibly defensive. They surround themselves with an impenetrable shield. Even friends are pushed away — friends who, more than likely, will not bring the situation up again.

In the EXCITEMENT phase, I did not see any difficulty in the opportunity ahead of me. Now, I see difficulty *everywhere,* and *very little work gets done.* Plenty of unforeseen problems appear — problems that would have seemed trivial six months ago. Because of my defensive shield, I won't seek any help or assistance. As a result of this negative anger state, I contribute to my problems instead of identifying or seeking a solution. As my anger and frustration continue, I will eventually decide that I'm not going to work here any longer. This decision seems to make all of my problems disappear.

But now I have a new problem: I have to rationalize my commitment to you. Remember when I excitedly accepted your job offer? I start thinking back to our initial job interview, when you and I talked about this opportunity. You probably asked me, "Jim, can you handle this?" And my response was, "Absolutely!" You might have even said,

"What I'm really looking for is a strong-minded self-starter who can take on challenges without a whole lot of support." And I said, "You've got the right person."

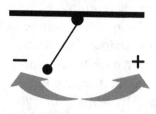

JUSTIFICATION

MOMENTUM CONTINUES

To further reinforce your po-sition, you may have added, "You need to understand that in some cases, we won't be there to support you when you need us. You'll just have to keep marching through the difficulty until we can give you some help." My response? "I can walk through hot coals. Don't worry about me."

Now here I am, not wanting to walk through anything that you and I have talked about. I no longer want to fulfill my original commitment to you. To get out of that commitment, I drop into another subphase called JUSTIFICATION.

5. JUSTIFICATION

I *do* realize, subconsciously, that I made a commitment in the beginning. Even so, despite what I may have promised you originally, I have no desire or intention to take care of my obligations. I start compiling a list, mentally or other-wise, to justify my feelings and my decision. I may even seek additional negative input and reinforcement at this point. In this subphase, my attitude pendulum swings completely into the negative area, and it begins gaining speed as I start piling up blame.

First, I would probably blame you, my boss. After all, you got me into this mess. But I won't tell you. I'll just know in my mind that you're part of the cause. I might even mention to someone else that I think you're part of the problem.

FULL JUSTIFICATION

FULL TILT NEGATIVE

To further justify my feelings, I begin to list every thing and every situation and just about every person — *except me*. I might list

... the political changes that cause a certain amount of fear and concern;

... or how the secretaries won't type my reports on time;

... or how the accountants won't let me spend the amount of money I feel is necessary;

... and, of course, the designers and manufacturers are behind schedule in delivering the goods.

Not only that, but the economy has changed ... the job has changed ... my family commitments have changed .. what *we* have to offer is not as good as what *the competition* offers ... and so on. I'll list every negative drawback I can think of, regardless of how small or nitpicking it might be. In my mind, these are valid reasons for not moving forward, although you and I both know that they are nothing but flimsy excuses.

I continue to add to my list of justifications. Like jelly beans on the pan of an old-fashioned set of scales, my pile of excuses gets bigger and bigger and bigger until I finally convince myself to give up. For some people, it only takes three or four jelly beans. Others pile on 15 or 20 before they give up.

This justification subphase *has to be there* because of my original commitment to you. In my mind, I will remain committed to you until I can pile enough reasons on the scale to overcome the weight of that commitment. When I succeed in doing this, ACCEPTANCE sets in.

6. ACCEPTANCE

In the ACCEPTANCE subphase, I decide and mentally accept that I am no longer obligated to meet my original commitment. I am still working for you, and I may continue to do so for years, if you allow me to, but I am apathetic and uncommitted. I'm in a sort of mental semi-retirement state — no gold watches, no testimonial dinners, no celebration — just mental retirement. Everybody knows it. I throttle back, and the rest of the staff picks up the workload. Things move along as usual.

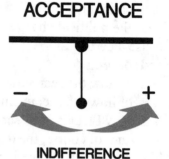

I don't throttle back enough to cause myself to be removed, of course, but most of my real energy goes to activities other than my job. I'll spend more time at the golf course, visiting with friends, or working on my hobbies — anything I can do to remove myself mentally from the frustration of the job and the commitments I made to you.

Accepting my "impossible" situation makes things easier. Releasing myself from my commitment to you eases my burden and relieves the pressure I've been feeling. My hope for a better, brighter future allows the *totally* negative outlook I had in the justification stage to become somewhat mollified. My attitude pendulum can thus ease back to the neutral, uncommitted, indifferent center.

In this subphase, there is no momentum in my attitude at all. At the beginning, I was totally and enthusiastically committed. *Now I am indifferent and much less productive than*

I could be.

A real tragedy is taking place. This was the perfect opportunity for me, remember?

Why isn't it working out?

Why am I throwing it away?

SPLIT SECOND CHOICE

Chapter 4

The Third Phase: LOOKING

"One ship drives east and another west, while the self-same breezes blow
"'Tis the set of the sail and not the gale, that bids them where to go.
"Like the winds of the sea are the ways of fate; as we voyage along through life,
"'Tis the set of the soul that decides the goal, and not the calm or strife."

Ella Wheeler Wilcox

To escape my FRUSTRATION, I begin LOOKING for a way out.

LOOKING PHASE

This third phase, which I call LOOKING, is where I start to find out what other opportunities might exist for me. It begins with scanning the want ads, or maybe checking with friends in the industry. To keep you, my boss, from finding out about my inquiries, I will do it all in a third-person manner.

I will go about my normal business, occasionally saying, "I have this friend who is looking for a job. Have you heard of any job opportunities lately?" If an opportunity presents itself, I will explore it (discreetly, of course). I might even engage some professional help — in a very low-key fashion — from a recruiter.

I have completely reversed my attitude towards my situation. In the beginning, I was absolutely sure I had entered the most fantastic opportunity in the history of mankind. Now, I am absolutely sure that coming to work for you was the worst decision I ever made. Why? I was lied to, and things were misrepresented. It just didn't turn out the way I expected. (Or so I have convinced myself.)

It is this logic that propels me into LOOKING for a brand new opportunity: another opportunity having the same criteria I thought my position with you offered. Why? So I can get back into an EXCITEMENT phase again.

Psychologists say that we naturally gravitate toward happy situations. People will work to find what makes them happy, and they will make a change, regardless of the cost. Leave me unhappy long enough, and I will clear the decks to make a new start.

It may take time, but I will continue to look. As a matter of fact, I have talked with people who stayed in the LOOKING phase for as long as 20 years. They literally became a ward of their employer. In a large organization, one can hide for a long time. At some point, the organization may even know that you're unproductive, but it's easier to allow you to muddle your way through to retirement than to go through the difficulty of removing you and developing someone else.

Most of the time, I will look to similar industries for my next job opportunity. And it won't be hard to find something because at this point, I have experience. I will eventually find something that seems to meet my needs. I will probably describe it as another ground-floor opportunity — the career position I *should* have had — the most fabulous opportunity one can imagine.

This time, when such an opportunity comes along, I will take extra care in interviewing the company. I will check its background, its financial stability, the people within the company and even the boss (both personally and with respect to company matters). Because of my experience, I now know what I should have asked during my interviews with you. I ask a thousand more questions than I did with you. I make sure to get lots and lots of information. Once I've convinced myself I have the information I need — that this new opportunity is really what I've been looking for and not another mistake — then I make a decision to go with the new company.

I now come back to you, my boss. Before telling you about my decision to move on, I tell you what a great person you are and how wonderful your company is. Why? Because all my life, I've been told not to burn bridges.

Instead of being disappointed, you are relieved. You know I am not productive, and you may have been wondering what to do with me, anyway. So after telling me how much you enjoyed the relationship, and how much I've meant to you, you wish me luck in my new endeavor. You encourage me, saying things like, "Hey, that sounds like a great opportunity. Looks like it's really your cup of tea." Under your breath, you're probably saying, "Thank heaven, this is no longer a problem for me." Of course, your feelings don't really matter, because *I'm sure YOU were the major cause of my problem,* anyway.

Off I go into my new career opportunity. It's important to note that my goals haven't changed — I have merely walked away from my first career opportunity unfulfilled.

But that's okay, because I am back in an EXCITEMENT phase again, telling my family, friends and even strangers what a fabulous, once-in-a-lifetime opportunity I have seized and am holding fast in my grasp. This is it!

My attitudinal pendulum swings back to its positive pole.

Remember, psychologists say that you and I will naturally gravitate back towards a happy situation. Looks like I've found one, doesn't it?

Questions for you to ponder at this moment are, "Will I be okay?" "Is this the one for me?" "Is this the career I have always been looking for?"

Chapter 5

The Cycle Repeats

"Follow me. I'll be right behind you."
Anonymous

Now that I have found another company to work for, and another career, I am excited again. How long will I stay in this "new" EXCITEMENT phase? You are right! Three to six months. Then, suddenly, I will find myself out of EXCITEMENT and back into FRUSTRATION.

Why do you suppose that happens? This was truly *the* opportunity. I checked this company out much more carefully. I asked so many extra questions. How could this possibly happen again?

Let's examine the situation in more detail.

Do you remember the list I used to justify dropping my commitment on the first job? Even though I am honest, chances are good that I did not list myself, or even consider myself to be any part of the problem. I blamed everyone and everything else for my problems.

Well, read carefully, because here is your explanation. Even though I may not be the direct cause of the problem, I am the only person who can do anything about the problem. That's so important it ought to be repeated. *I am THE ONLY PERSON who can do anything about the problem.* I hold the solutions. I hold all the cards. Even though I cannot control every aspect of every situation, I do have the power to choose a negative or a positive attitude.

I've heard it said that half the people you tell your problems to don't care about them. The other half are glad you have the problem and they don't. Either way, they leave the problem in your lap. *Bottom line: We have to take responsibility for solving our own problems.* When you understand that, you can easily understand that if I am not on the justification list — if I don't consider myself part of the cure or responsible for part of the problem, and if I don't take personal action to make positive changes — the cycle will continually repeat itself.

When the SHOCK strikes this time, do you think it will be greater or less than before? You're right! My SHOCK will be greater. I may be stunned at how two separate companies could be so closely allied in trying to ensure that I fail at everything I ever attempt in life.

Do you think my DENIAL subphase will happen more quickly? Or will it take longer? You're right! It will be immediate. That is how I protected myself last time. So I'll do it again. Right away. I will quickly back out of the stream of responsibility.

The FEAR subphase. Greater or less? You're right again. Tremendous fear! Especially if this is my third or fourth time through the cycle.

A couple of years may have gone by — maybe five. I think to myself, "I cannot continue to change careers (or companies). I just can't. If I continue to do this, I will eventually reach the end of the line, without anything really worthwhile to pursue." Adding to my concern is the fear that at some point, when I'm older, the job opportunity I'm really qualified for will come along but I'll be competing with a much younger man or woman. All other things being equal, will I get the job? Not likely! Even with equal qualifications, and more experience, I'll probably lose out to the younger person.

The ANGER subphase. Will it be more vivid? Stronger? More intense? Absolutely. You're right! I immediately surround myself with anger. This way, I can push away anyone who might help me. It's just human nature to do that: It's a simple human tendency to push help away. Pride enters, too, keeping me from asking for help and virtually ensuring that I will make yet another wrong decision. I may even act like I know everything, even though I really don't.

Now, JUSTIFICATION. Will it be easier, or more difficult? Right again! It's easier, because everything looks familiar. I simply pull out my old list and place a check mark by things that apply to my new situation. A handful of new names and stories are added, and the list is done.

ACCEPTANCE sets in quickly, too. It's the same old story. I can easily accept the idea of having been sold down the river again, misled by those I thought were telling me the truth, lured back into the same old trap.

I immediately shift attitudinally into my LOOKING phase, where I begin looking for yet another opportunity. If I have been caught up in the cycle several times, and much of my life has passed, then this might be my final opportunity to find what I really want.

Normally, as we are organization or career shifting, we will stay within our chosen career field, especially if there are plenty of job opportunities. If the opportunities are scarce, we may have to relocate to maintain the same career pursuit. Sometimes, we have to completely shift careers, moving and changing our line of work. Many people find themselves scanning the want ads on a regular basis. They are constantly shifting and moving. The problem with this is that they never stick with anything long enough to really excel.

I may go through the cycle dozens of times without even realizing that I am swirling through it. Discouraged by repeated FRUSTRATION, I then apply the negative cycle described in Chapter 3 to my own dreams and goals. Goals and dreams I had when I was young now seem unreachable. SHOCKED at this discovery, I begin to DENY that they were ever possible in the first place. With the FEAR of what might happen if I continue to reach, but fail, I become ANGRY at the world.

Along comes JUSTIFICATION to convince me that all of this is somebody else's fault and that I am doing better than most of the people I know. After convincing myself that I have more than most, I rationalize that my opportunities were probably just pipe dreams. JUSTIFICATION makes it easy for ACCEPTANCE to set in: acceptance of easier goals, shallower dreams and lower standards.

This was the story I heard from the hundreds of people I interviewed. As they grew older, they grew "wiser," deciding that some of their original goals and dreams were unrealistic. They reasoned that most of their goals were set by others and that they had never really been personally committed to attaining them. Rather than continuing to develop themselves, they simply reached up, grabbed the high objectives they started out with and pulled them down to their current level of performance. Then, without being truthful to themselves, they said, "I'm satisfied with what I've accomplished. It's all I really wanted, anyway." They went on spending the rest of their lives on a mediocre performance level, a level unnecessarily and unsatisfyingly low.

When a person goes through this cycle time and time again, they will often begin to develop a distorted perception of reality. They start finding fault with people who do well. They criticize our society and systems. They become very cynical, and unhappy, maybe to the point of never being happy again. They say, "Everybody else gets the lucky breaks. I'm a good person, but I never get a break!" Once people decide the rest of the world is lucky and they're not, they usually stay unlucky for the rest of their lives.

THIS CYCLE CAN BE LETHAL. IT CAN CHOKE THE LIFE OUT OF CAREERS, PROJECTS, PERSONAL COMMITMENTS, MARRIAGES, SPIRITUAL GROWTH, FINANCIAL GROWTH, COMMUNITY WORK AND EVEN YOUR HEALTH!

A young man working for me actually taught this attitude cycle in workshops, yet he didn't recognize the stages developing in his own career. He denied that it was true in his case. (Denial is one of the subphases of FRUSTRATION, remember?) He commented that his was a different situation. I must admit there were some differences, but the cycle was still there, choking the life out of his career. Despite the advice given to him and his understanding of the cycle, he made a career change, and then another career change, and the last I heard, yet another one. Meanwhile, a new man took the same territory and excelled.

As you read this, you might be saying, "Wait a minute, Jim. I'll admit there are plenty of people, including many successful people, in the world who have an 'attitude problem,' but they don't seem to be caught up in this lethal cycle. How do you explain that?"

One answer is that many people are simply stuck in the LOOKING phase, permanently mired in an uncommitted, medium-level production mode. They have simply ACCEPTED their FRUSTRATION as a way of life.

There is also a more subtle explanation that I can best illustrate by example. One day, at the beginning of a training meeting with a large oil field organization, a man raised his hand and said, "I want to identify myself. I'm the one that everyone always cuts a wide berth around." (In other words, he was admitting that he had an attitude problem.) I thanked him for his honesty and went on with my program. As we began to toss more ideas around, he made another interesting comment: "In our organization," he said, "it doesn't matter what your attitude is like. If you're skilled enough, you're tolerated." (Here he was trying to say that his attitude problem didn't matter.)

I suppose we can reach certain levels of skill where even a miserable attitude is tolerated because those specialized skills are hard to find. Of course, a miserable attitude doesn't guarantee failure, but it sure increases the odds. The reverse is true, as well. Having the right attitude doesn't guarantee your success, but it does make it more likely.

If you're fortunate enough to be one of those highly skilled people who can't be replaced, then perhaps you can go through life and accomplish a few things, perhaps even most of your financial goals. However, it's unlikely that your relationship with your family and your associates will be ideal. It's also unlikely that you'll reach the top of your field, be promoted into upper management or elected to a leadership position.

A big challenge this country faces is that average, and sometimes even mediocre performance is rewarded quite well. We can do a mediocre job throughout life and yet own a nice home and a couple of cars, have a pretty good lifestyle and raise our children. In other words, it is relatively easy to "succeed" without reaching for one's maximum potential.

After reading this, you might be saying to yourself, "Well, it's too late for me. I'm too old to reach for high goals now." Not true! Many of our world leaders are in their 60s and 70s. Plenty of people are working into their 70s, 80s, even their 90s, setting and achieving new goals all the time.

We choose when to shut it down — which means we also choose when to gear it up.

Colonel Sanders began his Kentucky Fried Chicken chain when he was more than 65 years old. Not only that, but he was turned down by hundreds of restaurants when he first attempted to sell his recipe. Think of the FRUSTRATION he must have experienced! Yet he succeeded in the end.

Inventor Thomas Edison tested thousands of different materials for the filament of his electric light bulb. Many of them failed completely, and yet FRUSTRATION did not send him looking for another profession. Why? The next two chapters will offer some insight into the way these men, and many others, managed to prevail in the face of such attitudinally defeating odds.

At this point, it would be worthwhile to go back and read this chapter a second time, then perhaps even a third. After that, take some time to think through the situations in your life that were similar to the ones described — times when you may have walked away from a commitment unnecessarily. Think about circumstances that were seemingly bad when you left them and how, when looking back, don't seem quite so bad. Were all of the reasons you gave yourself for walking away really valid? Think this through before moving on to the next chapter, and take heart because you can break the negative cycle. We choose the direction of life's journey. It is our choice to make.

SPLIT SECOND CHOICE

Times I Walked Away

_____
_____
_____

Why I Walked Away

Valid?
Yes   No
□   □
□   □
□   □

Times I Stayed Committed

_____
_____
_____

Why I Stayed Committed

_____
_____
_____

HOLD IT!

WAIT A MINUTE!

TIME OUT!

WHOA!

STOP!

You mean life doesn't have to be a frustration trap?

SPLIT SECOND CHOICE

Chapter 6

Breaking The Cycle: Your Choice

"Let us grasp the situation. Solve the complicated plot.
Quiet, calm deliberation untangles every knot."
Sir W.S. Gilbert

"Many of life's failures are men who did not realize
how close they were to success when they gave up."
Thomas Edison

To this point, we have been looking at how careers, projects, marriages and many other aspects of our lives can spiral out of control. It's time now to break free of those chains and make some progress.

Not everyone continues to change jobs or says, "That's it, I quit." We must admit that many people do, but not everyone. Some people never seem to quit. Like Colonel Sanders and Thomas Edison, they achieve great things in life, and the roads they are travelling usually aren't any easier than ours. Frequently, there are even more obstacles in their way. How do they do it?

The answer, in large part, is that they avoid the negative side of the cycle.

The negative side of the cycle doesn't have to happen. We can break free from the helplessness. We can break free from the hopeless feelings — that everything we touch dies — that we kill relationships and opportunities and talent. This doesn't have to take place. We can break the cycle. You, me, all of us, have *the liberating power of choice.*

Breaking the counterproductive cycle is similar, in many ways, to the way we avoid collisions. For example, if you knew that backing out of your driveway tomorrow morning would cause you to land right in the path of an unyielding garbage truck, would you do it? If you knew that the garbage truck was going to smash broadside into your car at a high rate of speed, total your car and injure you, would you go out of your driveway in that manner? Or would you find another way to leave your house? *OF COURSE YOU WOULD.* You'd even drive over the backyard fence and through a rock-covered, pothole-infested field to get to work. *YOU WOULD FIND A WAY TO AVOID THAT COLLISION.*

We avoid most collisions in life because we know what to look out for. We can see the obstacles in our way and steer around them.

An attitude collision is not as easy to see coming. It doesn't just show up in front of us. We must learn how to look for it. What we need is some kind of mental guidance system — perhaps a large mental flag, waving and saying, "Danger! Danger! Self, you need to make some different choices and make them now!"

Well, get ready, because it's time to sew that flag.

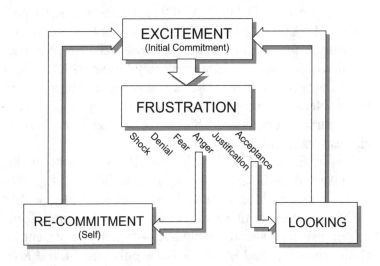

ATTITUDE POWER

To understand how to become part of the solution instead of part of the problem, let's break the cycle down into its component parts.

EXCITEMENT is first. It is the most productive phase. During this phase, our attitude and enthusiasm are high. We get many things done. Our commitment is solid, and things run smoothly. This is where we want to spend more of our time.

Because obstacles always confront us, FRUSTRATION inevitably follows EXCITEMENT in all of our long term commitments and in many of our short-term commitments, as well. It is here, in the subphases of FRUSTRATION, that our attitude begins to slip. Our enthusiasm begins to decline, and our commitment begins to deteriorate. Perhaps this is where we should begin looking for the way out of our attitude problem? Ironically, this is exactly what we do.

When we allow FRUSTRATION to overpower us, we proceed to the LOOKING phase to escape. *LOOKING is the phase we want to avoid, because **it carries us away from our original objective(s).*** We can never totally avoid FRUSTRATION; however, it is here that we can choose to be a part of the problem and complicate things, or we can choose to become part of the solution. This choice belongs to us. No one else can make the decision for us.

To stay EXCITED and avoid LOOKING at other options, the answer must lie in the way we handle FRUSTRATION.

Let's take a closer look at the subphases of FRUSTRATION. Looking at those subphases — shock, denial, fear, anger, justification and acceptance — which one presents a choice to us? Right! ANGER is the only one. ***ANGER is the signal that we're about to get into attitudinal difficulty.*** We need to see this coming. Just like backing out of our driveway and looking for other cars, we need to be looking for ANGER!

Okay. We know what cars look like, but how do we recognize anger?

The subphases of SHOCK, DENIAL, FEAR and ANGER seem to follow each other naturally and unavoidably. In fact, most of the time, their effects are so subtle that they blend together. How can we identify the exact time and place to make our choices? Fortunately, it is not critical for us to be able to recognize a specific point of time. We need only to be able to recognize the ANGER.

For most of us, ANGER usually manifests itself *in an outward manner.* It can be as simple as a minor feeling of irritation. It could show up with something like gritting our teeth, clinching our fists, cursing a lot or blaming the boss for a problem at work. Or perhaps we find ourselves in a gripe session with fellow workers. This kind of anger is difficult to catch, but we can catch it if we are alert to the signals.

More often, ANGER is expressed in forceful ways, ways which are more obvious and easier to note. We may find ourselves closing the car door a little bit harder. We might slam the door to our house or office when we walk in or slam our books down on the table. We might drop our toothbrush in the morning, then throw it across the bathroom just because we dropped it. We may find ourselves hollering at somebody when we're driving in traffic, or we might snap at our spouse or one of our children. Anything that triggers our temper or puts us out of emotional balance can be the signal flag we're looking for.

We need to be on the alert for these seemingly unimportant signals. These signs of ANGER — some subtle and some not so subtle — can indicate to us early on that we'd better put the brakes on and make the right choice for continued success, or we could be facing a major problem.

But what is the right choice? *The right choice is choosing positively directed anger instead of inwardly or outwardly directed anger. We have to turn our ANGER towards positive solutions to avoid an attitude collision in the outside world.* This is the choice of champions and Super Achievers.

Remember, the ANGER subphase is a precarious position for us. It is the point where we make split-second decisions, and habitual choices. These are learned responses. This means that we will usually respond unconsciously to the stimuli, reacting the way we have been trained to react.

One of the ways we might respond when we feel angry is to direct the anger outward. With outwardly directed anger, everyone and everything is the cause of our problem — everyone, that is, *except us*. As we have seen, this rationalization response is usually unproductive and quite often leads to

JUSTIFICATION, ACCEPTANCE and LOOKING. When we do not take any responsibility for a problem, we are refusing to participate in the solution. We are leaving it for others to resolve.

Another way we might respond is to direct the anger inwardly. *With inwardly directed* anger, we might say, "I know I'm the problem. I'm no good at anything. I'm worthless." This type of approach is self-destructive.

The **best** response, or choice, usually lies in *assuming personal responsibility* for our frustration, then following through by redirecting the energy of our ANGER towards a positive solution. We put blinders on horses so they can only see what's in front of them and thereby avoid distractions. We humans can benefit from a similar strategy. In a sense, we want to blind ourselves to the possibility that a*nything or anyone* could be RESPONSIBLE for the SOLUTION(S) to our problems except us. This will help keep us from simply blaming others for our circumstances and cause us to look toward *real solutions* for our frustration.

Normally, we will want to rechannel our energy by recommitting to our initial goals. This, and other ways of responding will be discussed in the pages that follow. For now, it's only necessary to recognize how POSITIVELY FOCUSED ANGER can be one of the most powerful tools we have to keep ourselves marching towards our goals for ourselves and our families.

I didn't completely understand how anger could be used in this positive, productive way until I reflected on my experience with rheumatoid arthritis.

Many years ago, I was serving in the Marine Corps and stationed in Japan. I was a long way from home, family and friends. For three months, I found myself locked in a full body cast, getting weaker each day and watching my weight drop by more than 40 pounds. My doctor told me, "Jim, you need a medical discharge. You're never going to walk again. Even if you manage to walk for a while, you will be crippled at 35 and confined to a wheelchair from that point forward." I didn't know what to think. It looked as if the doctor might be right. But somewhere deep in my spirit, I just knew I could not allow that to happen. I didn't want to be shipped back to the naval hospital in California, either. He continued to push me toward a medical discharge, and I continued to refuse the transfer.

Eventually, I was sent to therapy, where I consulted with an elderly Japanese physical therapist. I wish I could remember his name because he represented a wonderful, refreshing experience for me. In broken English, he asked me, "You want walk?" I looked at him in shock. No one else had asked that question. They had only told me that I would not walk. Not knowing anything else to say or do, I just nodded my head affirmatively. He lit up with a smile, and said, "Okay. You walk." I'll never forget that moment.

That day started a six-month process of physical therapy. I actually had to learn to walk all over again. But what a joyful experience. His daily encouragement focused not on where I was, but on where I would be if I continued to make the right choices. So, I kept making those choices, as painful and difficult as they were, and exactly 13 months from the day I entered the hospital, I walked out on my own two feet. I could not do a deep knee bend and get back up without support, but I was able to walk.

The doctor refused to give me light duty and sent me back to Okinawa, instead. He was still convinced I could not get well. My anger was so great that I wanted to knock that doctor's head off, but privates do not strike captains in the Marine Corps without winding up in the brig. He must have felt that I would give up and ask for the medical discharge. I decided to prove him wrong. Every morning, I got up early to exercise and strengthen my legs. Six months later, I was marching 15- and 20-mile forced marches successfully. And today, well past the 50-year marker, I'm still able to walk and run.

The tragedy of this experience was that I went through the pain of recovery to prove the doctor was wrong, not to get well. As sad as that may be, it taught me a great lesson. I learned that anger, focused with a positive intent, is one of the most powerful tools we have to make changes, to exercise choices, to turn our dreams into reality. Used in a positive way, we can focus the energy of our anger to achieve whatever we need to achieve.

As noted above, we'll be discussing more about how to focus our anger in a positive way in the chapters that follow. Right now, it's important to add another point. *We can't always see anger coming. We might not even recognize it when it arrives.* Sometimes, we blow right through ANGER into JUSTIFICATION, which is where we really start blaming others for our problems. That's okay, in fact it's even good, because *it offers us yet another opportunity* to make the right choice. If we can't catch our anger *on the front side* of the decision point, we can still catch it *on the back side.* Then all we have to do is back up a little bit and steer our attitude in the right direction.

In summary, if we can see the negative use of anger coming, or catch ourselves directing anger at other people and organizations, then we can refocus and redirect its energy. We can catch our attitude pendulum before it swings to the negative, and send it back to the positive. Accomplishing this will keep our attitude positive, our enthusiasm channeled in the right direction, and our commitment level high.

You are probably saying to yourself, "Okay, fine. I see how to catch myself, and I see how ANGER can be a positive force. But what can I do to redirect it towards a positive solution? How do I redirect my attitude? How do I drive my pendulum back towards the positive?"

Remember Colonel Sanders? What do you think he did when he was turned down for the hundredth time? What do you think Thomas Edison did each time he tried a filament that didn't work? Here's a clue:

When we make the right choice during the anger subphase, our problems are half solved.

We can avoid the deadly LOOKING phase if we want to. It is our choice. We can travel through a fourth phase, instead, and totally bypass the LOOKING phase like other successful people do. In the next chapter, I will show you how right choices make this cycle work for you instead of against you.

Before moving on to the next chapter, this would be a good time for you to stop and think for a moment about the times in your own life when you were up against tough odds. Did you respond by directing your anger in a way that made positive results take place? There are probably many cases where you took positive directional control. I am confident in that assertion because if you were not already a winner, you would have stopped reading this book long ago.

TIMES I USED POSITIVE ANGER AND SUCCEEDED:

_____

_____

_____

_____

_____

_____

_____

_____

_____

_____

Chapter 7

The Fourth Phase:
RECOMMITMENT

"All of the significant battles are waged within the self."

Sheldon Kopp

OKAY, IT'S SOLUTION TIME.
BUT REMEMBER, YOU ARE THE
ONLY HOLDER OF THE KEY.

YOU, AND ONLY YOU,
ARE RESPONSIBLE FOR YOUR
ATTITUDINAL DIRECTION IN LIFE.

Let's start the cycle all over again. We'll keep the same set of circumstances, but this time, we will direct ourselves down the POSITIVE path of the cycle.

You're my boss again, and we start off in the same way. You interview me three times, and you also interview my spouse. You offer me the job, and I accept it. With my acceptance comes my initial commitment. I don't know how long my commitment will last, and you don't know, either, but it looks like a win-win situation for both of us. I start to work for you, seeing my job as a great opportunity. Things go well for a period of time.

This EXCITEMENT phase is "just right" and doesn't need to change. At the beginning of any commitment, project, career or relationship, we will find some measure of excitement. If we cannot find some value and personal reward at the beginning, we should not, and probably would not, start the process.

Also note the positive way that I see the job: I see it as a great opportunity. This positive dream of my future can and will help me get back up on the tracks after I fall off.

Reality doesn't change, either, and within three to six months, I will shift into a FRUSTRATION phase for some reason. SHOCK will strike. I will DENY responsibility. FEAR will loom. ANGER is ready to strike, too, but this time, I will respond differently. (Remember, we will never be able to eliminate FRUSTRATION, but positive choices at the moment of truth can direct our energy favorably instead of unfavorably.)

So, here I am. I'm SHOCKED at the difficulty of the job. I DENY it's my responsibility, and I shift some responsibility to you, my boss. At this point, I become FEARFUL it won't work out and that I might fail. ANGER strikes, but instead of directing the ANGER in an unproductive way, I say, "Self, you've got a problem." And at that point, I take all of this powerful energy — one of the most powerful energy forces we have — and I focus that energy towards a solution instead of complicating the problem. The right decision is to choose personal responsibility for my own situation, my own attitude, my own destiny — to take charge and make positive changes.

POSITIVE CYCLE

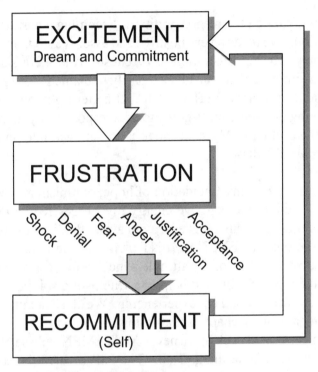

I begin a more productive, alternative phase of my journey during this split-second decision in the ANGER subphase when I say, "No way. Not for me. This is not going to be outwardly directed ANGER. *I'm not going to blame other*

people. I'm not going to feel sorry for myself, either, but I am going to look inside of myself and ask, 'Where or what can I change? How can I strengthen my position? How do I get *myself* back on track and back into another EXCITEMENT phase?'"

By taking on the responsibility of becoming a part of the solution, I've made a very positive and assertive step towards dealing with my frustration or its cause. And there's a bonus: Admitting that I am at least partly to blame for my problems has a cleansing effect. I'll feel better right away just knowing that someone is going to take responsibility for solving the problem. My next move is to get back into an EXCITEMENT phase.

How?

Starting with my foundation of hope, optimism and courage, I redirect the negative energy my FRUSTRATION is producing. I channel this energy in a way that gets me back into the positive EXCITEMENT phase, where I can refuel the booster rockets of my attitude. Once there, I can also productively search for, and help construct, solid solutions for any *real* frustration I am experiencing. We'll talk about what that means in the chapters that follow.

To get myself back into a new EXCITEMENT phase, there are several simple things I do. They all involve the same general action concept, which is to *recommit myself to my vision and my goals.* This is why I have labelled the fourth phase RECOMMITMENT. I have found three helpful steps in this RECOMMITMENT phase:

1. RE-DREAM THE DREAM

In many ways, people are like the old-time, steam-driven locomotives of the 19th century. Remember the way those engines just kept chugging down the tracks? Until they ran out of steam, that is. For humans, dreams are the fuel of the Enthusiasm Engine that powers our human locomotive. To carry a full head of steam at all times, we need to keep our mental engine full of dreams.

Whenever I find myself in the ANGER subphase and running out of steam, my first step toward correction is to sit down and ask myself, "Why did I start this commitment or career or relationship (or take on this opportunity or project) in the first place?" The initial thoughts I have concerning a commitment are healthy, positive, inspiring and uplifting. Remember chapter one and the EXCITEMENT phase? Remember the dreams I had and how I saw that particular career as the perfect career for me? Now is the time to review those thoughts.

I ask myself:

"What was my dream?"

"Why did I choose to commit myself?"

"Why was the excitement there?"

"What result did I want from that situation or dream?"

"Who else was excited about it?"

I make sure I think back and re-experience the positive feelings I had, the vision and sounds of success, the reasons and motives behind everything I chose to do at that time.

Each time I mentally revisit those dreams, I cause my finish line, or victory party, or desired reward, to look better than it did before. Usually, this thought process alone is enough to renew my spirit, cancel out much of the FRUSTRATION I am experiencing and propel me right back into a new EXCITEMENT phase.

Almost every book or tape on attitude or achievement tells us to believe in a successful end result. They suggest making mental pictures, or visualizing each step of our intended activity in order to strengthen our performance. This is what super achievers and champions do. They re-dream their dream frequently as part of their training and competitive conditioning. Virtually all Olympic gold medal winners describe their state of mind just before and during competition as one of simply living out their dream. This human ability to see a desired goal and then make it happen is one of the most powerful aspects of human motivation.

As long as the dream is clear, alive and healthy, our attitude helps move us toward the achievement of that dream. When the dream gets cluttered, foggy, fuzzy or hard to see, then we start focusing on the obstacles in front of us. When that happens, our attitude becomes a faulty part of our internal circuitry and helps burn us out instead of moving us forward. Our EXCITEMENT begins to diminish, and FRUSTRATION replaces it. It is critical for us to keep our dreams clearly in front of us.

You've heard the old saying, "He couldn't see the forest for the trees."? Here's another experiment for you. Find a large, wall-mounted mirror, and put the book down. Hold your right hand out to the right, and extend your left hand to the left. Looking in the mirror, focus both eyes directly on your right hand. Now, without losing focus of your right hand, look at your *left* hand. Be sure to keep looking at your right hand! Of course you can't do that. **It's impossible to focus on two things at once.**

As a wise hunter once said, "A dog can't chase two rabbits." We must choose to follow the dream, not the difficulty. If we focus on the difficulty, we will spend all of our energy fighting instead of progressing.

How about trying another experiment? Find a penny. With your left eye closed, put the penny between your thumb and forefinger, and hold it close to your face in front of your right eye. What do you see? The penny. And that's all we're going to see. When we focus on the difficulty of the situation, we will not see the goal any more, and we will stay frustrated.

Our choice has to be to pull that penny aside. Why? When you pull the penny aside, what do you see? The whole world is in front of you. Don't let insignificant, petty circumstances act like that penny and block your vision from the wonderful opportunity you and I have in this life. The human race has more worthwhile projects and goals in front of it than ever before. They may be challenging to see, but they are there, and they can belong to you when you make the right choices.

A wise gentlemen once said that "enthusiasm is the flywheel that carries your saw through the knots in the log." I interpret this to mean that we need to redream our dream every time we encounter a knot in our life, every time we encounter an obstacle that seeks to slow down the progress of our saw.

2. SHORT-TERM GOALS

Sometimes, my FRUSTRATION runs deeper than thoughts of success can overcome. When I need additional strength, I take a second step to get back in an EXCITEMENT phase. I call this step "short-term goals."

One of the reasons FRUSTRATION has taken a strong hold of me is that I haven't experienced much success lately. Frequent success can make it easy to ignore occasional frustration, but repeated failures and setbacks have demoralized me to the point where I see only more failure in my future. I'm very discouraged, and that is why I am LOOKING to escape. Have you ever suffered through a success accomplishment drought like this?

I have to reverse this process. I need some success right away. The best way to get some is to start with a small success and build from there. I look for a place where I can set a simple, short-term goal and cause some success to happen.

Psychologists say that when we accomplish something, our brain emits an endorphin. It's like a pure form of morphine, and we wind up with a real lift in our spirit. What I need is to get my spirit lifted.

One way to guarantee some short-term success is to set up a series of one-hour projects — one for each day of the week or several for one day — that are fail safe. To give you an example of how simple this might be, let's assume that our car is so filthy we hate to admit it's ours. There may be some old candy wrappers inside, or a half-eaten apple underneath the seat, and maybe the internal odors are starting to over-whelm us. So we say, "That's it. Come Saturday morning, I'm going to wash that car."

At 10 a.m. on Saturday, we take on the project. We wash the car. We wax the car. We clean the mag wheels. We scrub the tires. We wipe newspapers on the windows to get the glass sparkling clean. We polish the chrome. We shampoo the carpets. We vacuum the trunk, and when we are through, the car looks better than the day we drove it off the showroom floor.

It's been a couple of hours, and we're hot and sweaty. We decide to go down to the convenience market and pick up a soda. When we get in the car, it seems to start more easily. It seems to run better. It seems to shift more smoothly. I've even had people tell me a clean car gets better gas mileage, because as the wind flows over the clean, unrestricted area of the car, it has less resistance. Ever felt like that? This is an example of how multiple benefits can stem from one success.

But let me ask you, what really changed? That's right. We changed. We set a goal and accomplished it. We successfully finished a project and got endorphins to lift our spirit. And with each successive project, we will find ourself winning and accelerating back into an EXCITEMENT phase.

Short-term success can be measured in terms of hours or even minutes, as well as in terms of large or small accomplishments. When working in a sales capacity, I can set a goal to make 10 prospect calls in a given timeframe, then get on the telephone and do it. If I'm experiencing frustration in my communications with someone, I can set a goal to reestablish or enhance communication, then call the person I'm having difficulty with in order to work toward achieving my goal right away. It's easy to set and achieve short-term goals.

Ideally, the short-term goals I choose should be related to my overall goal. It can really benefit me to clean my car when it helps move me forward towards a larger, more important objective, like working towards a sale with a customer who will be impressed by the cleanliness of my automobile.

What's the bottom line? Some action is needed to provide immediate success — to allow me to progress toward my dream. Success will help convince me that things are eventually going to work out in my favor. Success will lead to more success and get my pendulum swinging back in the positive direction.

The positive feelings that result from fresh success are usually enough to accelerate me right back into EXCITEMENT. But once again, I am the only one who can make things happen. No one else can take action for me. I must make that choice for me, and you must make it for you.

3. OUTSIDE OPINION

What if re-dreaming the dream and reaching some short-term goals are not enough? Whoa! Hold it! You mean, that may not be enough? Sorry to disappoint you, but the answer is yes. Sometimes, we need to take a third step. In many cases, this is the most difficult step to take.

Let's suppose that short-term projects lift me up some, but the FRUSTRATION is now so deep that I can't get myself back into that state of sustained EXCITEMENT where I'm really productive. This is when I go into my third step. I need a special person to give me some good, objective advice. I call it an "outside opinion."

I must look for the right person. *Most people simply will not do.* I need to find someone I can trust, someone who is impartial, someone who can give me sound advice. Ideally, I need someone who has successfully mastered a situation similar to mine.

Let me first identify some people who probably will not be helpful.

In my younger days, before she passed away, I might have called my mother. She loved me, and would do anything I asked her to do. If I were to call my mother, I would probably say, "I'm not very happy right now. I'm having a terrible time with my career, and things are not going well. The company is not doing what they promised to do. They're not treating me the way I thought they'd treat me. I'm not growing as fast as I want to grow. Things aren't changing like I want them to change. Mom, I'm so frustrated I can't stand it. Sometimes I want to just sit down and cry about how bad things are."

A mother will sympathize with her offspring. She will likely agree with everything I say. She might even make a phone call to you, my boss, and tell you to get off my case.

If I really sound depressed and frustrated, Mother might possibly say, "Quit. Get out of there. You're too talented for that. Why put up with it? You know you can do anything you want to. You were looking for a job when you found that one. They don't appreciate you."

But is quitting the answer? It may be, and we'll discuss that possibility later. For now, let's assume that quitting is not in our best interest. Since I don't want to quit, my mother's no help.

Who else can I talk to? I could call a couple of good friends or perhaps talk it over with my spouse. Would that be a wise thing to do?

If I call someone who loves me, they'll ask, "What's wrong?" I'll tell them my problems. Because they love me and are sympathetic to my feelings, they'll probably agree with everything I say. They may even take my side and join me in blaming the company or my boss for my difficulty. As a result, they're no help.

Of course, the only information they have is what I tell them. They naturally join my side because they only have my half of the story. During the early part of my career, I recall telling my wife all the things I was asked to do that I didn't like, but I never told her how right those things were for me after I did them. As a result, she only got half of the picture, and there was no way for her to feel good about my career the way I did because she didn't have all the information. And your friends won't, either. It's not likely we'll tell them the whole story because if we understood the whole story, we probably wouldn't be where we are attitudinally. If we understood completely, we wouldn't need their help.

And as my mother did, my spouse and my friends may even suggest that I take the wrong path to solve my problem.

That wrong path would be slipping out the back door like a thief in the night. Worse yet, I might agree and take a walk on that path, because it's easier to blame someone else and quit than it is to accept responsibility and lead myself out of trouble.

When I am locked in the FRUSTRATION phase, I can be so full of fear that my attitudinal clock will stop keeping correct time. It may even begin ticking backwards. I'm not thinking straight. Nothing I decide in this state of mind will be correct because I'm running down a blind alley. I think someone may even be chasing me. I'm running anyway, as fast as I possibly can.

F.E.A.R.
(FALSE EVIDENCE APPEARING REAL)

Fear such as that can only be destructive. But as the Chinese say, nothing is to be feared; it is only to be understood. I need to find someone who can help me understand. If I can't talk to my mother, my spouse or my friends, who can I talk to? I need to find someone who will be empathetic, not sympathetic — someone who can understand how I feel, but who won't actually share those feelings. This kind of person can help me out of the pit without falling in there with me.

THE BOSS

The best person to discuss the problem with may be my boss. After all, we both have many of the same goals in mind. Also, the expense of replacing me might be far greater than the cost of helping me make it through this difficult time. More likely than not, my boss will be thrilled to give me the support I ask for and need. So I must have the courage to approach my boss for help.

But what if I'm finding it difficult to talk to my boss? Perhaps I've tried before without success, or perhaps I don't feel like the boss will be able to help. Perhaps I don't think the boss can be objective and/or impartial. What can I do?

The Chinese have another useful proverb: "If you want to succeed, consult three old people." This is very appropriate advice for my situation. I need to find someone I respect, admire and trust. It needs to be someone who can be empathetic and put themselves in my shoes, yet give me advice that's positive and not negative; someone who might even tell me, "Hit the streets. Make some more calls. Get back in there. Talk to your boss. Hit it harder. Go to school. Reeducate yourself. Be flexible." In short, it needs to be someone who can wake me up to reality and set me straight on course again, someone who will encourage me to stay until I fulfill every single commitment I made. Let's count ourselves fortunate when we have a boss, spouse, parents or friends who tell us in kind, or perhaps even in firm ways to get a grip, quit whining and get back to work.

The real secret lies in getting advice from someone who is not emotionally involved with you or your problem. It may be someone higher up in your company or organization, or perhaps a personal friend who has it all together. It may even be a person in another organization that you seek out by asking around. People like this are often called mentors, or red-flag partners. If chosen carefully, they can usually provide objective and impartial help.

RED-FLAG PARTNERS

A red-flag partner is a person who knows my situation well and will straighten me out when I need it. He or she can be an impartial friend, an objective co-worker or simply a helpful person in a position similar to mine — a person who knows which questions to ask. (Make sure they read this book so they'll know.)

Red-flag partners are generally there for emergencies, to help us get past a crisis. When you raise the red flag, your partner is there to listen and to help. After listening to your concerns, this partner shakes you awake, takes you back to the first step under recommitment and says, "Okay, let's talk about your dream. What are you trying to accomplish?"

Your red-flag partner controls the conversation with questions, and you allow it to happen. They listen while you explain again what you are trying to accomplish, with even more vivid detail, more clarity and more color. (The purpose here is to get that dream solidly back into your mind where it can pull you forward.) Then, he or she will walk you through step two of the recommitment process and help you set short-term goals. (Be sure to write the goals down, and ask your partner to hold you accountable for achieving them. Better yet, hold yourself accountable for the results, then send a thank-you note or gift to your partner.)

Your red-flag partner may also be able to suggest some creative ways of eliminating your frustration. Since you are in an emotional state, and he or she can remain objective, this person may be in a better position to see the forest instead of the trees. We need to listen carefully to objective, caring people. Pushing our emotions aside for a moment may be difficult, but that's what we need to do.

Since FRUSTRATION is inevitable, wouldn't it be a good idea to find a red-flag partner early, before FRUSTRATION strikes? Of course it would. It's best to identify a red-flag partner when both you and your partner are in EXCITEMENT phases. It's also good to make very strong commitments to help each other in times of difficulty and to have more than one such partner. And if they aren't available at the moment you need them, they know to get back with you quickly if you leave a message that it's about a serious communication.

MENTORS

Counselor. Guide. Teacher. Tutor. These are all synonyms for the term mentor. Each one suggests that a mentor will point us in the right direction and help us learn.

Students of the martial arts often refer to their instructor or master as "sensei." Sen means "before," and sei means "born." Thus, the literal meaning of the term is "one who is born before." While the instructor is often an older individual, the real meaning of being "born before" lies in the wisdom the master possesses. Presumably, the master has experienced what the student is going through and has successfully mastered the task. At least he or she should know how to help the student master it.

A mentor can be a very powerful ally during our periods of FRUSTRATION. Since this person is "older and wiser," he or she should be able to guide us through the forest of FRUSTRATION and back into the green grass clearing of EXCITEMENT. Remember, the best mentor is someone who has been there or has successfully navigated the rough waters we are facing. That's where our best advice will ultimately come from. By seeking out people who have avoided frustration, surprises and negative experiences, we can learn how to avoid problems ourselves.

The right mentor provides guidance, direction and, most importantly, wisdom — a strong and steady hand — a rock or shelter for stormy times. Sometimes, just asking ourselves what the mentor would say is enough to help us. No matter how much experience we have, a mentor is a good thing to have. Nowhere is this better demonstrated than in the martial arts, where even the masters have masters.

The objective advice I receive from a mentor or red-flag partner and the encouragement given to me are almost always enough to turn my commitment, my enthusiasm, my attitude and my excitement around. Chances are high that you won't need to leave that company, situation, project, marriage or relationship. Why? Because everything you ever dreamed of is still there, just like in the beginning. You are merely camouflaging it with negative thinking born of FRUSTRATION.

RECOMMITMENT STRENGTHENS US

POSITIVE CYCLE   NEGATIVE CYCLE

POSITIVE CYCLE	NEGATIVE CYCLE
EXCITEMENT	EXCITEMENT
FRUSTRATION	FRUSTRATION
RECOMMITMENT	LOOKING

Once we make a positive move out of FRUSTRATION into RECOMMITMENT and rise above a particular situation, is it likely that the same set of circumstances will put us back into FRUSTRATION? No, it's not likely. The same set of circumstances cannot stop you; however, a variation of those circumstances could have another frustrating impact. But having successfully mastered the first situation, we are in a better position to work our way out of the second.

Each time we go through the cycle, each time we hit that wall of frustration and we fight through it, we get stronger and stronger and stronger. Of course, if we don't fight through it, we get weaker and weaker and weaker.

The net result of the four-phase cycle is this: We can repeatedly follow the negative cycle, getting weaker and weaker, eventually having to lower our expectations in life. Alternatively, we can repeatedly **CHOOSE the positive path of the cycle and continuously get stronger.** Through continuous recommitment, we can begin to reach out and accomplish greater goals and greater expectations, some higher than we ever dreamed possible. We can use our knowledge of this cycle to our advantage.

IT'S YOUR CHOICE!

We know that FRUSTRATION is a natural part of living and part of the learning process, so we cannot avoid it completely. Am I able to avoid FRUSTRATION after all these years of working with the concept? Absolutely not. I try to move quickly on to recommitment, using the frustration as a strengthening process. Each time my runway is bombed by frustration, I rebuild it with the stronger concrete of renewed commitment and enthusiasm.

Every time frustration slaps us in the face, we ought to say, "Thank you. Thank you! This is an opportunity to make some real progress, and now is the time to get started." Plunging in and recommitting with enthusiasm kicks us right back into a high level of excitement and productivity. As Confucius said, "Men's natures are alike: It is their habits that carry them far apart." **Recommitment is one of the best habits we can form.** It is a habit that will carry us to great horizons.

FRUSTRATION is merely a temporary storm passing through our lives, while EXCITEMENT is the rainbow in a clear blue sky. FRUSTRATION always passes back into EXCITEMENT, but unlike the rage of foul weather, it's our choice as to when. Cycling back into EXCITEMENT makes us feel good. And as is the case with the weather, we will always be able to see and be awed by the beauty of the rainbow after a storm.

STOP!

STOP!

STOP!

Do yourself a favor, and read this chapter two more times.

First time	☐
Second time	☐

Then find a red-flag partner and a mentor.

Red flag partner	☐
Mentor	☐

NOTES ON MY EXPERIENCES:

_____

_____

WHAT I HAVE LEARNED:

_____

_____

SPLIT SECOND CHOICE

Chapter 8

Dealing With
FRUSTRATION

"So, you think you know everything, but you don't know the difference between an inconvenience and a problem. If you break your neck, if you have nothing to eat, if your house is on fire, then you have a problem. Everything else is inconvenience. Life is inconvenient. Life is lumpy."

Sigmund Wollman

Up to this point, we have been looking at how the complete cycle of attitude fits together as well as the two main attitude paths that people follow (see the diagram at the end of chapter 7). Now it's time to consider some specific issues that can help us put our newfound understanding to work. In this chapter, we will take a closer look at the subject of frustration. Since the FRUSTRATION phase is where our attitude train jumps the track, we can benefit by preparing ourselves to handle frustration in the best possible manner.

THE NATURE OF FRUSTRATION

Webster's dictionary defines frustration as a "deep, chronic sense of insecurity arising from unresolved problems." This definition makes frustration sound like a severe psychological disorder requiring the advice and care of a physician. If your experiences are this severe, then I would encourage you to consult your doctor; however, for this book, a milder version of this definition should be sufficient. Let's define frustration simply as a sense of insecurity arising from unresolved problems. In this way, we can deal with the garden variety of frustrations ourselves and leave the really troublesome, chronic ones to doctors of psychiatry and medicine.

Armed with this definition, we can begin to investigate the nature of frustration. First, we know that frustration is universal: Everyone on earth has to deal with it. Like eating, breathing and sleeping, frustration is a natural part of living. Second, we know that frustration is inevitable. We cannot avoid it. Third, we know that frustration produces uncomfortable feelings for us, often leading to anger. Finally, and most importantly, we know that frustration is a product of the human mind. (When it grabs us and takes us for a ride, it is only because we have given our permission.)

Frustration is associated with experiences ranging from quickly forgotten nuisances, irritations and disappointments to heavy-duty, exasperating, constantly present aggravations. Minor irritations, like burning a piece of toast every once in a while, are easily dismissed. We can shrug these off most of the time. But if the irritations or problems continue, frustration can build into a much bigger, more difficult to resolve, emotional problem.

For example, the irritating actions of young children are usually minor when examined individually, but they can add up rapidly to produce strong feelings of anxiety, stress and anger in everyone around them. Similarly, we know that when couples first fall in love, they often overlook minor conflicts and annoying behavior. Over time, however, frustrations can accumulate, leading to deep feelings of hurt or anger. Longer, sustained periods of frustration cause people to quit their jobs, divorce their spouses and abandon their life's dreams. In extreme cases, the cumulative effect of unresolved frustration can lead to deep-seated illness or perhaps even suicide.[1]

FRUSTRATION TOLERANCE LEVEL

Each of us has a "frustration tolerance level" that we have developed as a result of life's conditioning process. For most of us, the level is reasonably high, allowing us to deal with at least one source of stress. As long as the water in our frustration tank doesn't overflow, we can periodically drain the tank and experience relief. However, when frustrations rain down upon us regularly, or from multiple sources, or when the drain line is plugged, our tank can overflow, leaving us to deal with a flood of emotion.

As we have seen, frustration overflow can cause major problems with our attitude. The accumulation of sufficient irritants at work or in our relationships is what ultimately leads to the FRUSTRATION phase of our attitude cycle and its various subphases: shock, denial, fear, anger, justification and acceptance.

The flood of negative emotion presents us with the choice we have already reviewed at length: We can react constructively to the flood, or we can react destructively. In most cases, RECOMMITMENT is the constructive response, and it can help us counteract the negative emotional effects of FRUSTRATION.

We will be even better prepared to defend our attitude if we can somehow prevent an attack of frustration in the first place, or eliminate the frustration once it occurs. This is the focus of this chapter. To head off frustration, or to eliminate it once it has begun, we have to understand what causes it. When we zero in on a cause, we can take action to neutralize it.

WHAT CAUSES FRUSTRATION?

Remember our definition? Frustration is "a sense of insecurity arising from unresolved problems." In our careers, an acute level of frustration overflow develops when we feel out of control — when too many unresolved problems pile up. This can happen quickly if the results we are getting do not measure up to our expectations or if our achievements are falling short of our goals.

Our inner being is designed to bring our actions into harmony with our controlling thoughts, similar to the way an autopilot tries to keep an airplane on course. Just like airplanes, we do not have total control over all of the things that affect us. Airplanes have to deal with foul weather and other airplanes flying around. Pilots can enter erroneous headings, and enemy forces can shoot destructive missiles. So even with the autopilot, planes can crash.

Planes occasionally crash, and so do people. Since we cannot stay in control at all times, we will experience periods of frustration. When we can get our achievements back up to where we want them to be, the frustration goes away. On the other hand, frustration that is allowed to linger and fester like an untreated wound often leads to the negative attitude cycle we have already discussed. Like an airplane out of control, we crash.

In relationships, both at home and in the workplace, frustration develops primarily over unmet expectations. One person expects another person to behave or perform in a certain way, and when that doesn't happen, feelings of aggravation develop. We feel uncomfortable because we cannot get the other person to change or to act within our desired timeframe. This relates directly to our need to be in control. When we are in control, everything is fine. When we are out of control, we are frustrated.

RESPOND IN A POSITIVE WAY

At times, you may be in a position of wanting to keep the job you hold or wanting to maintain a relationship, but you are feeling very frustrated. You are feeling a need to relieve the pressure of the frustration pressure-cooker because it has paralyzed your effectiveness or your relationship. If this is where you are, you have recognized your frustration, and that is a major accomplishment. You know where you are in the attitude cycle, and now you can choose which path to take. (You will take the positive path, won't you?)

FIRST STEP

Your first step towards eliminating your frustration is to step back emotionally from the feelings of frustration. Since the wrong emotional response to frustration is the true enemy, we have to prevent our emotions from going awry. We must fight to stay in emotional control while we decide how to respond to the irritation(s). As we will see, irritation can stem from real or imagined sources. It is important to note that regardless of the source, we can choose to deal with frustration in a positive way. Whether we make the decision consciously or unconsciously, this is the choice we want to make.

SECOND STEP

Once we have made the decision to stay in control of our emotions and to constructively focus them, we can begin to identify the specific cause of our frustration. We can start with a series of questions:

What is irritating me? (See text box, next page.)

Why do I feel the way I do?

Is it because I'm dissatisfied with my own performance?

Is it because others are putting pressure on me?

Is there an obstacle in my way that someone can remove?

Is it because someone else hasn't done something that I wanted them to do?

Is it because someone won't act the way I want them to?

Is it because I need someone to relieve me for a while?

Is it because I'm in over my head and need some help?

Are my standards of performance too high and in need of adjustment?

Am I trying to be perfect in an imperfect world?

Am I expecting perfection from others?

These questions, and others like them, help us identify the things that are causing us to feel so uncomfortable. Patience, time and effort will usually lead us to some good answers. I try to be completely honest with myself, and it isn't too difficult because I don't have to share my feelings with others unless I deem it appropriate.

It's also important to look for more than one cause. Since the cause or causes may be subtle and hard to discern, it may help to write out the answers or to draw diagrams. It can also help to rank them numerically, by priority or by impact. With some answers in hand, we can proceed to another question.

THIRD STEP: IS IT LIVE, OR IS IT MEMOREX?

Several years ago, a television commercial featured the voice of an opera singer shattering a crystal goblet. The question raised by the announcer was, "Is it live, or is it Memorex?" The manufacturer was making the point that recordings on Memorex tape were just as real as the live performance. Or more to the point, that the listener wouldn't be able to tell the difference. In the same way that opera performances come in both live and re-

---

TYPICAL IRRITANTS

Noises
    Babies or young children
    Ringing telephones
    Motorcycles and trucks
    People talking
    Boom boxes and car stereos
Traffic
Crowds
Family
Delays
Information overload
Insufficient information
Disagreements
Lack of cooperation
Rapid change
Work overload
Improper tools
Inadequate knowledge
Insufficient funds (money)
Interruptions
Car trouble

---

corded versions, the obstacles that cause frustration come in two varieties: real and imaginary. For each one of the causes we have identified, we need to ask ourselves, "Is this a real obstacle in front of me, or is this an imaginary obstacle?" Knowing the difference will enable us to choose the most effective response.

If the obstacle is real, then we can begin to work systematically to remove it. An example of a real obstacle might be a sudden surge in the number of customers you have to deal with or a deadline that got changed without negotiation. It might be as simple as the need for a new piece of equipment — one that works reliably. Perhaps someone else in the department really isn't pulling his or her weight. In a relationship, it might be the sudden realization that the other person is dishonest; or, you may recognize the existence of activities that make achievement of your personal goals impossible.

Each of these obstacles can be confronted in a physical sense. We can get help to deal with the customers. We can renegotiate the deadline. We can purchase or lease a new piece of equipment. We can remove the person who isn't pulling his or her weight. We can choose how to more effectively interact with a dishonest person. Finally, we can work around, or perhaps remove, any activities that are preventing us from achieving our goals.

If the obstacle is imaginary, then we will need to resolve the problem in our own mind if we are to remove it. Imaginary obstacles include personal feelings of inadequacy, a feeling that someone in the organization is out to get you when they really aren't, feeling pressured to achieve a goal that seems impossible, or feeling that you are all alone in your task. The common denominator in these imaginary obstacles is F.E.A.R.: False Evidence Appearing Real.

We want everything to go well, but we are unable to clearly see the future. Because we are fearful, we mentally project worst-case scenarios. When this is done vividly enough, or often enough, these scenarios grow more powerful. Eventually, the negative scenes drown out the positive ones. Then, our most feared case becomes the outcome we truly expect to see.

Let's look at an example.

Dinah Nicholson is a top-producing sales representative for a national financial services firm. She was asked to respond to the phrase, "If I knew then what I know now... " This is what she wrote:

"I would have been better prepared for those brick walls you keep coming up against in the beginning. I call them 'learning walls' or 'psychological walls.' Like the wall you hit when you've worked hard, done everything exactly right and all of sudden, you get total rejection. The thing I learned about walls was that each time I hit one, there was something — usually an attitude — that I had to change. Fear of failure, fear of success, fear of not being good enough. That first year, all our personal weaknesses come out, and we have to say, 'Okay, I'm not perfect. What can I change? What can't I — or won't I — change?' The most successful reps I know are the ones who have faced those walls, asked — and answered — those hard questions and adjusted their attitudes accordingly."[2]

Remember, "Nothing is to be feared. It is only to be understood." As Dinah figured out, it was the way she was responding to the stimulus that needed changing, not the stimulus itself. She had to adjust her thinking. She had to understand the fear and decide consciously that it was false evidence. With that understanding, she was in a position to move forward and become one of the company's top representatives. Note, also, that she decided to change herself — her own attitude — rather than trying to get the world around her to change.

Even when the concerns we face are imaginary, most of us will argue that the obstacles are real. We know, intuitively, that dragons are imaginary and that we shouldn't be afraid of them. So, we will do everything we can to create a REAL obstacle — even if this means lying to ourselves — and rationalizing that an imaginary obstacle is real. To make sure that we are actually facing a REAL obstacle, we should seek confirmation from someone else or by doing some research. If we can prove the obstacle is real, then we can work to remove it.

FOURTH STEP - THE CRITICAL FACTOR

Once you have clearly identified what is causing your frustration, ask yourself, "Would my frustration go away if *this* cause did not exist?" If the answer is no, you need to think more about what is causing the problem because you have not yet identified the root cause.[3] When you can answer yes, ask yourself, "What can *I* do to eliminate the cause?" Or, "What *must* I do to eliminate the cause?"

If you are having trouble digging out the root cause of the problem on your own, then seek out your boss or others in your company who are older and wiser. Present your problem in a positive, solution-seeking way. Try to get a variety of opinions and possible solutions, but be careful to avoid sharing your frustrations with too many people. Numerous well-meaning employees have been forced to change jobs because of the negative ways they went about seeking change.

When you have some answers in hand, work to eliminate the critical factor causing your frustration. You can use one or more of the following steps:

1. Eliminate it yourself, if you can. Make a behavioral change, or change the way you think about something. (See chapter 6 and the RECOMMITMENT Phase.) Take action to fix the equipment, or buy the equipment you need to get the job done. Move things around to prevent bottlenecks. Take a course in computer programming, time management or shorthand. Work harder, longer or smarter — but get the obstacle(s) behind you.

2. If you can't eliminate it by yourself, can someone else do it for you? Whose help do you need? Can your boss remove it for you? Your business partner? A co-worker? Another team member? Your spouse? Your children? Prepare a mutually beneficial proposal, then talk with them. Negotiate a solution, if possible,

but at least get the problem on the table, and ask for their help. Usually a partial solution is better than none at all. And generally speaking, the more heads, the better, when you are looking for alternative solutions. (Caution: Be careful not to accuse, or otherwise offend, the person whose help you are seeking.)

3. Get some outside, professional advice. This can help you invent a solution or a creative way to approach and solve the problem.

4. Once you have eliminated the cause of your frustration, make a quick pit stop in the RECOMMITMENT area, then head back out to the EXCITEMENT track.

Confronting your frustration and anger by taking the kind of constructive action just described is a crucial step. It is often difficult to approach a boss, a partner, a spouse, a customer or a child, especially when they are a big part of the problem. Sometimes, it takes determination and tenacity, but *it has to be done.* Remember, however, to **confront in a constructive manner.** I will address this issue in more detail in the next few chapters.

WRONG AND RIGHT RESPONSES

One of the wrong ways to handle our frustration is to mishandle the anger we are feeling. It is a mistake to camouflage our anger by faking harmony, remaining silent or covering up with gooey sweetness. It is also unwise to suppress your anger and allow your frustrations to accumulate in an unresolved anger tank. The energy from these suppressed feelings can manifest itself in other forms, such as guilt, obesity, insomnia, psychosomatic illnesses, backaches, dermatological conditions, headaches, gastrointestinal symptoms and ulcers — even sexual problems and fatigue.[4]

We also know it is almost always a mistake to be overtly angry. Unless you have an alterior motive, public criticism is the wrong kind of confrontation for anyone to make. It is also a mistake to be a closet critic — to harbor an undertone of anger, hostility and negativism. Neither one of these approaches will get you promoted, and they may even get you fired without explanation.

I once knew a promising young executive who was confident that he was right and the company was wrong. He made the mistake of telling several people high up in the company how he felt. A couple of months later, they offered him a choice between leaving or being put out to pasture where his opinions wouldn't matter anymore. He chose to leave. So even if he was right, he lost out on a promising career because he didn't reveal his anger in a positive, constructive, solution-oriented manner.

There is an ideal way to handle anger, and a very mature person will attempt to handle it in this way. It involves a combination of things. First, he doesn't save up anger stamps, and because of this, he has dealt with all of the previous anger in his life and his unresolved anger tank is empty. He doesn't hold anger inside where it can be destructive to himself, either.

Second, his response to irritating factors is by choice rather than by reaction. It is a controlled, somewhat delayed response.

Third, he is principle driven. This means that he is willing to get visibly angry, but only when injustices are done or other people's lives are at stake.

And fourth, his anger leads to positive action. He constructively dissipates his anger in a way that harms others the least yet leads to positive results.[5] Very few of us will ever approach this ideal, but at least we have something to work toward.

PREVENTING FRUSTRATION

As we have noted several times, frustration is inevitable. We cannot completely prevent it. Just like ants at a picnic, it is always present, even in the positive side of the cycle. But we can take steps to prevent it from occurring too often, and we can reduce the number of things that cause us to have feelings of frustration.

In my experience, the people who make quantum leaps in reducing the amount of overall frustration in their lives are the ones who work hardest at time management. Over a period of time — sometimes weeks, sometimes years — they somehow determine what really matters in their life. They sort through their basic beliefs and values and goals. Then, they spend their time working at activities that support those beliefs, values and goals. This focus allows them to minimize the non-meaningful events in their lives, thus increasing the feeling of satisfaction and decreasing the frustration associated with waste and wheel-spinning.

Another thing we can do is work at increasing our frustration-tolerance level. We can stop trying to be a perfectionist, if that is our calling. We can let more things go by without criticism or complaint. We can try to better determine what is really important and worth being concerned about. These suggestions are often grouped under the heading "Keeping Things in Proper Perspective." If your standards are too high, or your reference points are too specific, you may be setting yourself up for a lot of extra frustration in your life. I'm not suggesting that you lower all of your standards, just the ones that won't make a critical difference in your life. We can pursue excellence without demanding perfection at every turn.

Parents can help their children become more successful as adults if they will work to increase the child's frustration-tolerance level. When it is clear that a child is in the FRUSTRATION phase, then our responsibility is to coach them into, and then through, the

RECOMMITMENT phase. In this way, we can show them how to successfully and systematically work through the obstacles in their lives.

Supervisors can help their associates by anticipating frustrating events or changes and helping their employees cope with the event or the transition. We can also coach our associates into and through the RECOMMITMENT phase. I'll have more on this later.

REOCCURRING FRUSTRATION

If our frustration keeps reoccurring, it is even more important to make a thorough analysis of the cause of the irritation. If we have been attacking the wrong cause, then the frustration will keep returning. We may also be facing multiple causes at the same time, which can cloud our ability to clearly see the root cause or causes. It might be beneficial to work with someone skilled in cause-effect analysis, or perhaps a trained counselor, if this is what you are facing.

As we know, the biggest problem with frustration is the negative consequences that can emanate from the emotional feelings of shock, denial, fear and anger. With prolonged frustration, we will build up a considerable amount of hostility and indignation. If we simply reject these feelings over a long period of time, our unconscious mind will take control and totally eliminate the feeling part of the process. When we switch our emotional responder to "autopilot" in this fashion, the anger can be manifested in many different forms. We may not feel anything, or we might simply feel numb, hurt, disappointed, irritated or annoyed. Anger that is repressed in this fashion will ultimately seek expression in some sort of aggressive, defensive or destructive manner against either ourselves or others. So it is important to get some help and work towards an effective solution.

SUPPRESSED (MUTED) FRUSTRATION

You may be one of the many people who is trapped in a career or relationship that does not utilize your talents to the fullest. You may have unknowingly placed yourself within a comfort zone where you are able to tolerate the level of frustration you experience. If this describes your situation, then you may find it very hard to maintain yourself in an EXCITEMENT phase because you aren't working towards much of a dream. My best advice to you would be to think about what your dreams really are and to begin working towards them. As Seneca, the Greek philosopher, noted, "When a man does not know what harbor he's making for, no wind is the right wind."

Our goals must be clear. This may mean changing careers, making new friends, dropping long-cherished beliefs or even getting a divorce. When a car proves itself to be a lemon, it's time to get a new one.

OVERCOMING FRUSTRATION

All of us have experienced some degree of adversity in our lives, and all of us have overcome it with a variety of achievements along the way. The degree to which we recognize those achievements and give ourselves credit for our ability to overcome adversity will play a large part in defining the level of self-confidence we will be able to call upon when we have to deal with the next set of frustrating experiences in our life. Keep a file or a list of the achievements and successful experiences in your life, and refer to it periodically as a reminder that you can succeed.

RECOGNIZING YOUR OWN STRENGTHS

Think back over your life at this point, and make a note of some of the challenges you have faced and successfully overcome. Write your strengths on the Personal Assets Form in this chapter. This exercise will help you realize that you *do* have the ability to deal with frustration successfully. It will help you discover where and how you have successfully dealt with frustration before.

You might also test the concepts in this book as you go along. When you have improved your ability to deal with frustration, you will be ready to move on to more challenging assignments, higher goals and greater fulfillment. You will be on your way to becoming a Super Achiever.

PERSONAL ASSETS FORM

A challenge I successfully faced and overcame was:

_____

_____

I dealt with the FRUSTRATION phase of this challenge by:

_____

_____

The specific strengths and personal abilities I showed in doing so were:

_____

_____

[1]Dwight Carlson, M.D., **Overcoming Hurts & Anger** (Harvest House Publishers, 1981), p. 27.
[2]**Waddell & Reed World**, Vol 35, No. 2, February, 1995.
[3]The root cause is the cause from which all other causes stem. The problem you are facing might be attributable to many different causes, but there is probably only one cause that, in turn, causes all of the other causes. You need to keep digging until you find the root.
[4]Carlson, p. 26.
[5]Ibid., 60-61.

Chapter 9

Commitment: Your Secret Ingredient

"Desire is the key to motivation, but it's the determination and commitment to an unrelenting pursuit of your goal – a commitment to excellence – that will enable you to attain the success that you seek."

Mario Andretti

"Individual commitment to a group effort — that is what makes a team work, a company work, a society work, a civilization work."

Vince Lombardi

"Commitment is what transforms a promise into reality. It is the words that speak boldly of your intentions. And the actions which speak louder than the words. It is making the time when there is none. Coming through time after time after time, year after year after year. Commitment is the stuff that character is made of; the power to change the face of things. It is the daily triumph of integrity over skepticism."

commonly attributed to Abraham Lincoln

COMMITMENT RULES!

Let me congratulate you. If you have read this far, it shows you want to succeed, and you believe in seeing things through. On the other hand, if you simply turned to this chapter, you are either curious, or seeking a specific result and operate with efficiency in mind. Either way, you have some admirable qualities, not the least of which is your quest for ideas and techniques that will improve your life and your results.

So – let's talk about application of the Split Second Choice concept in a place where it can help you hit not just a single or double, but *a whole series* of home runs – your career.

As we begin – keep in mind that even the best home run hitters don't hit a home run every time they come up to bat. That's a critical distinction – because you don't have to be perfect in order to have *great* success. In fact, contrary to popular slogans, **failure IS an option**. Failure is what provides us with the feedback to correct our course and get on the right track to success. And without failure, we wouldn't know what success really was, because we wouldn't have anything to compare it to.

As you know from previous chapters, the subphases of Frustration provide signals that you are off-course, and need to make a "course correction" back into Excitement. To understand this better, let's consider the career beginnings of Bill and Sam.

Both go to work for the same company. Both have 10 friends and relatives they can call on to get started in their profession, and talk about potential business. Both are excited, committed, and determined to succeed.

Bill jumps right in, and eagerly sets an appointment with one of the 10. He figures he can learn something by doing something, and that he can just correct any mistakes he makes on this first appointment when he moves on to his second appointment.

Sam, on the other hand, is concerned that he might make a mess of his first opportunity if he is not fully prepared for the interview, so he decides to study all of his materials before setting an appointment. Allowing for all the contingencies he might face, he buries himself in preparation. He wants to be perfect when he goes on that first interview because he believes that will give him the best chance of success. He is so concerned about his performance, that when he finally does set the appointment and goes on the interview, he gets all flustered when things don't go perfectly, and he blows the opportunity anyway.

But he's not sure why he did.

At this point he becomes *even more* concerned. He doubles his preparation and study, and even takes time off from work to calm down a bit.

Meanwhile, Bill has taken *his* determination to succeed and moved on to his second, third, and fourth appointments. He is "learning to do by doing," and he is getting better with each experience, because failure *is* an option for Bill.

Sam may eventually catch up to Bill and succeed – if his commitment is strong enough to overcome his anxiety and allow him to persist.

On the other hand, Bill *is virtually guaranteed to succeed* because he simply corrects his mistakes when and if he makes one. Bill takes personal responsibility for any frustration he is experiencing, and recommits to improve his performance on the next call. If he were a basketball player, he might be saying to himself, "Okay, so I missed one. Give me the ball and let me take another shot. I'll make the next one." This is recommitment in action.

Sam is using different self-talk, saying something like, "This is a lot harder than I thought it would be. I'm not sure I can make this thing work. Why didn't someone tell me it would be this difficult?" In making the choice to talk to himself this way, Sam is outer-directing the anger he feels, is blaming someone else for the challenges he faces, and is not taking personal responsibility, nor recommitting. He's not quite there *yet*, but it won't be long before he's looking for a way out of his chosen career.

Some of this behavior is personality driven, and your personality may well determine whether you approach your career like Bill or like Sam. But Bill's approach will generally get faster results, and Sam will usually frustrate himself and any supporting cast he might have, until he gets angry, makes the wrong split second choice, justifies his failure by blaming his circumstances or other people, goes looking for a way out, and quits.

A log on a railroad track can stop a powerful locomotive dead in its tracks. While both Bill and Sam started out with a good attitude and a healthy commitment to success, Bill let his excitement carry him over, around, and through the mental logs on his railroad track, but Sam allowed those mental blocks to hold him back and slow him down.

Sam can change if he wants to, by making the right split second choice.

Making the right split second choice is choosing to channel your emotional energy (anger) in a problem-solving direction, by accepting personal responsibility for the problem, not blaming yourself or anyone else or making excuses, and recommitting to move the problem out of the way.

Tennis player Billie Jean King nailed it when she said, "Champions keep playing until they get it right." That is obviously Bill's philosophy, too. Sadly, our friend Sam doesn't even want to play until he is sure he can play a perfect game.

What Billie Jean *didn't* say is that champions also do a lot of things wrong along the path to becoming a champion. Those are the things they need to get "right."

Translation?

In order to win, *you start by going out on the court,* and you *keep going out on the court even when you've been losing or making mistakes.*

Failure *IS* an option, and *we should actually look forward to some failure because of what it will teach us.* Short term failure helps us get to long term success.

Problems and frustration are inevitable, *even for champions.* How you deal with them is what turns ordinary people into champions.

Putting Sam and Bill aside for a moment, let's get back to you.

Let's assume you've just started a new business with "XYZ Company." You decided to go into this business because the products and services the company offers are top-notch, high-quality, clear-as-a-bell winners. You know this to be true because of what the products have done for you, or for others. They are so good that everyone who finds out about them is going to want to buy them in order to get the benefits they provide. You see yourself winning every award the company has to offer, and quickly rising to a position of high income and respect.

Almost by definition, you are EXCITED about this DREAM opportunity, and also by definition, you are COMMITTED to your own success. And well you should be – because IT *IS* A DREAM WORTH GETTING EXCITED ABOUT AND COMMITTING TO!

Well, for a little while maybe.

Is this being cynical? Perhaps. But for a good reason. It *is* a dream worth getting excited about, and *it will be* worth committing to *if you are planning to RECOMMIT to your DREAM every time* – and I mean *EVERY* time, you experience frustration. And *only* if you do, because otherwise you'll quit before you realize your dream.

Without recommitment, you not only fail temporarily – you fail permanently.

That's a choice for you to make – a split second choice – to recommit (and eventually achieve success), or go looking (accept your failure). And you can make it *now*.

Decide *now* to make that choice every time you need to make it, and *pledge to yourself that you will do whatever is necessary to fulfill that choice* each time it reappears.

Now back to your career move again. Let's be realistic for a moment and examine *your* attitude. Just what are you excited about? And how deep does the river of your commitment run?

Are you excited about the money you can make? About the rewards you can earn? About the honor and respect and position power that high achievers obtain? All of the above?

Or maybe you're running away from something, like a previous job you didn't enjoy, or a big pile of bills you need to pay?

Either way, you have the motivation to succeed. But be honest with yourself. Is it really your dream and your vision to make all that happen? Or is it just a wish (a wish is something you'd like to have, but don't want to make any sacrifices to get)?

If it really is just a wish, stop reading, go find yourself a solid, tangible, attitude-sustaining dream, and come back to finish this later. If you have trouble coming up with a dream for yourself, go hang around a dreamer for a while and learn how to dream for yourself.

Since you're still reading, we can safely assume you've got a ready-to-wake-up-in-the-morning-and-get-started DREAM. Your vision of success is clear as the picture on a high-definition television, and you can see yourself winning all the prizes.

That's good. A clear, compelling dream is *more than half* the battle. The rest of your challenge will be your committing to that dream, and committing to believe in yourself.

So the next question is, are you truly committed? Check yourself on a scale of 1 to 5:

1. I guess so. I'm here, and I'm reading this.
2. I'm gonna give it a good try. I want this to happen.
3. Definitely. I don't see anything that could stop me.
4. I'm all in. Let's do what we have to do to make this work.
5. *Nothing can stop me* from making my dream a reality!

It's challenge time.

If you scored yourself a five, give yourself a pat on the back for saying the right thing at the right time. Give yourself a second pat on the back if that commitment is unshakeable, because *that one promise to yourself will make all the difference* – when you keep it.

But now let me ask you another question – what are you willing to sacrifice right now, today, to make your dream succeed?

Would you spend your life savings to buy what your mentor says you need for success in this business? Would you put your family on hold and tell them you won't be around much for the next several months, or maybe even a couple of years? Would you tell your friends you can't go to the game, play golf, have lunch today, go shopping? Would you call a hundred people in a row and ask them for something, and be willing to stand on a mountain of "No's" in order to get one "Yes"?

I hope you were able to answer yes to all of those questions, because the stronger your commitment, the more likely it is you will succeed. With anything less than an absolute, take-no-prisoners commitment it is *possible* to succeed, and some people do because there are exceptions to every rule, but it also means *you are leaving yourself an "out."*

When Julius Caesar ordered his army to cross the Rubicon River in 49 BC he violated the law, and in effect, declared war against the Roman Senate. As the Army's leader, Caesar knew that if there was "no turning back," everyone would fight with absolute, irrevocable commitment. In other battles, many Greek armies had burned their ships after crossing water into a foreign land so that there would be "no turning back."

Is your commitment that strong? I'll ask you again - just how deep does the river of your commitment run?

Commitment is what makes RE-commitment possible. The stronger the *initial* commitment, the easier it is to recommit when necessary. A strong commitment is what you need. As Og Mandino once wrote, "Failure will never overtake me if my determination to succeed is strong enough."

While it is a fact that many top executives don't have any more ability than the next guy, they end up at the top because of an incredibly strong commitment. That commitment to a single purpose is what compels them to develop the habit of doing things that failures (quitters) just won't do. And unfortunately, it is also a fact that many people with brains and talent do not make it to the top of their professions simply because *they don't have the desire and commitment to make it happen.* They have developed the habit of escaping their commitments when it's convenient for them to do so. Parents inadvertently help their children develop this bad habit, and our news media glorifies "victims," so it's up to us to develop our own success habit.

Bottom line? *I can have all the talent in the world, but without commitment I won't use it. But with even a little bit of talent and a lot of commitment, I can be successful. My commitment is therefore more important than my talent.* That's just a fact of life. And the habit of recommitment is equally important.

As former president Calvin Coolidge once said, "Nothing in the world can take the place of persistence. Talent will not; nothing is more common than unsuccessful men with talent. Genius will not; unrewarded genius is almost a proverb. Education will not; the world is full of educated derelicts. Persistence and determination alone are omnipotent." What he was talking about can be summed up with one word: recommitment. Persistence doesn't take place without recommitment.

Frankly, most people today are just not as tough as the warriors of ancient Greece. It's hard to adopt a "no surrender" attitude unless you are fighting for your life. But you *can* increase your commitment to a level that will ensure success, if you really want to. We'll talk about how to do that in a moment, after we understand how to measure it.

MEASURING COMMITMENT

Many of us are what could be called "good intenders." We set good goals for ourselves, and we "intend" to accomplish them. Examples would include diet, exercise, and fitness. Business Coach Marshall Goldsmith has identified five reasons people do not succeed with their diet and fitness goals.

1. Time – it takes a lot longer than they expect, and they don't have that much time available

2. Effort – it's harder than they expect it will be, and not worth all that effort

3. Distractions – some sort of "crisis" emerges that prevents them from completing the program

4. Rewards – they get some immediate results, and some rewards and attention, but not as much as they expected, or as soon as they hoped

93

5. Maintenance – once they achieve a level of success, they discover "how hard it is" to maintain that success, so they slowly backslide, or even give up completely.

As you look at that list above, and think about your own business, do you see any parallels? Is the Split Second Choice attitude pattern evident? [Hint: FRUSTRATION takes the place of EXCITEMENT *in every case*, and no RECOMMITMENT takes place – so they go LOOKING, and end up quitting on their goal.]

One of the ways to increase, and then lock down your commitment, is to be realistic up-front about what dream fulfillment might require. Although many people reach their goals without doing an up-front assessment of all the challenges they might face, they usually don't delude themselves about the difficulties either. But let's face it, getting all revved up about a goal only to sputter out half-way around the track is just a big waste of time for everyone involved.

Commitment and motivation are quite similar concepts. When someone is not achieving, we frequently say "they just are not committed," or "they aren't motivated." Motivation is our "motive or reason for action," and commitment is "the state of being bound emotionally or intellectually to a course of action." We tend to use the term "commitment" at the outset of an endeavor, and then we refer to "motivation" as the endeavor unfolds, and if we maintain our commitment and motivation we call it persistence.

As John Maxwell says,

Motivation determines *what* we will do, and

Attitude determines *how well* we will do it

Let's add to that as follows:

Commitment determines whether we *will* do it, and

Recommitment determines whether we *keep on doing it.*

Bonnie St. John Deane, Olympic medalist in snow skiing, teaches a formula for motivation that can effectively serve as an ongoing measure of our commitment:

$$\begin{bmatrix} \text{Payoff} \\ \text{I Expect} \end{bmatrix} \times \begin{bmatrix} \text{My Odds} \\ \text{of Success} \end{bmatrix} - \begin{bmatrix} \text{Amount} \\ \text{of Work} \end{bmatrix} = \begin{bmatrix} \text{My} \\ \text{Motivation} \end{bmatrix}$$

Most of us use this formula intuitively to help us decide what level of effort we will put into something.

When we start a new business venture, we expect the payoff to be high, the odds of success to be high, and the work to be reasonable in relation to the payoff. According to the formula, our motivation would be positive, and possibly, quite high. This gets us EXCITED, and we COMMIT to take action.

Later on, as the FRUSTRATION of developing a new set of skills begins to appear, the potential payoff hasn't changed, but the amount of work required may be exceeding our initial perception. And if we've had a setback or two, our assessment of our odds of success may have dropped as well. It doesn't take a mathematical genius to see that our motivation has dropped. If we don't RECOMMIT at this point, we'll be in trouble.

Frustration and negative motivation will lead to anger (refer back to chapter 6), and if we let the anger be outer-directed we start playing the blame game or making excuses, and then – well, you know the rest of the story. We quit. Or if it's happening to someone you recruited into your business, *they* quit. Seldom will they actually call you up and say "I quit," but they stop working the business. It's the same for any business, organization or relationship. When people begin to lose their commitment, productivity slips away, relationships slip away, and lasting success will, too.

If you reach this point, it's not too late to save the day – although it might require some "heavy lifting" because the gap between where you are and where you need to be attitudinally has stretched so far apart. That's why the best strategy is to never let it get this far apart in the first place – which is why *regular recommitment (even daily) is so important to your attitude, and to your success.*

By measuring our motivation level using the formula above, we can effectively measure our commitment level as well. We routinely check the weather, the amount of gas in our car, and the value of the stock market. Maybe we should check our commitment level on a regular basis, too.

INCREASING YOUR COMMITMENT LEVEL

Now that we understand how to measure our commitment, let's look at ways to *increase* it.

Here are some strategies to help.

1. A clear and emotionally compelling dream is the starting point for commitment. Fuzzy dreams are weak, and dreams that are simply logical don't have much energy. If you want a high commitment level, start by working to establish a clear dream and vision of your future. Include your desired benefits, your future behavior, and your feelings about them. Passion is a force multiplier, so the more passionate you are about your dream, the better.

2. Experience your dream in advance. In The Success Principles, author Jack Canfield relates a story about how he was given a unique opportunity to *experience* his vision five years in advance. Invited to a "Come as You Will Be" party, he spent several hours pretending to be the successful author he later became. The event was staged with actors and actresses, and lots of imagination, but the effect on all of the attendees was

dramatic, with all of them achieving their vision within the next five years. Experiencing your dream in advance makes it stronger, and easier to recommit to when the going gets rough.

3. Re-dream your dream frequently. Schedule it on your calendar if necessary. Re-visiting an emotionally compelling and personal dream is like stoking the coals in a furnace. It re-ignites the fire and increases the heat. If a dream is the power that makes our attitude engine run, then re-commitment is the fuel additive that keeps it running at peak efficiency. As a leader, you can and should help others re-dream *their* dreams, to help *them* stay committed.

4. Finding bigger payoff's can help increase our commitment level. According to Bonnie's formula, a bigger payoff increases our motivation. Look for added benefits that will accrue to you when your dream is realized, and add these to your list when you re-dream your dream.

5. Do things that will *increase* your odds-of-success. While taking certain selective risks may improve your odds and your results, we are primarily looking for things that will increase our level of commitment in a sustainable way – teaming up with the right partner, improving your knowledge and skill in key areas, strengthening your relationships, working on the right things and doing them right. These are the kinds of activities that will help get the odds in your favor.

Instead of promising to make 100 prospecting calls this week, promise to make one. One is easier to do than 100, so your odds-of-success have increased. After you make the call, evaluate your results and consider how to improve on the next call, then promise yourself to make one call. This simple act, repeated a few times, will become a habit – a habit that will increase your odds-of-success, and prevent the stress that comes from unpleasant anticipation or overly optimistic goal-setting.

6. Get creative about reducing the amount of work required. Delegation is one of the biggest time and work-saving methods, because it leverages your personal time so effectively. As Archimedes said, "Give me a lever large enough and strong enough and I can move the Earth." Look for other ways to leverage your efforts, and look for ways to reduce or eliminate work that doesn't move you towards your vision.

Oftentimes our choice of focus is the key to reducing our work requirements. As a famous preacher once observed, "The secret of success is *singleness* of purpose." And later Benjamin Disraeli added, "The secret of success is *constancy* of purpose." So choose a single focus, and focus all of your efforts on that one thing. Eliminate distractions, and focus all of your energies like a laser beam on the one item of work that is critical to your success.

Focus is a form of commitment, and recommitment is simply refocusing, and thus concentrating your "eyes on the prize."

7. Take things one step at a time by setting some short-term goals, and tackling small, Fail-Safe projects. This increases commitment because we quickly begin making progress towards our long-term goals with short-term results. When you consider that a long-term goal is usually nothing more than a collection of short-term goals put together, this strategy can help you commit to achieving some *very* significant things. Books are written one page at a time, sales careers are built on one sale at a time, and lives unfold one day at a time.

We know that little things are easier to accomplish than big things, and that one step is easier to take than a thousand. As the saying goes, "Inch by inch life's a cinch. Yard by yard life is hard." Yet success guru Anthony Robbins has rightly observed that many of us are into "chunking." Instead of seeing a lifetime of fitness as a series of small steps, we mentally pile all the steps into one big pile, which seems insurmountable. It's like trying to carry a whole basket full of groceries into the house in one trip instead of making several smaller, easier trips.

8. When your tank of commitment is draining fast or running on empty, and none of the steps above will help, it's time to stop off at a commitment filling station and get your tank of commitment refilled. Good supervisors, red flag partners, and mentors usually have surplus commitment they can pump into your veins. Books and recorded messages can often serve this purpose, too, but *there is no substitute for the emotional connection of a face-to-face red-flag-partner discussion.* Tell your red-flag partner that your commitment level is dropping, and ask them for help. That's what you selected them for, and what they agreed to do when you first approached them.

9. Sometimes there are others around you who have a high level of commitment, and you can tap into their energy just by being around them, so *one of the best strategies* for developing and then maintaining a high level of commitment is to *hang around Committed and Excited People!*

When we are alone (and this can include being "alone" with our family), we are often cornered by our own negative-thinking habits, and fall into the trap of Looking for an easy way out of our Frustration. Escaping our commitments is an easy way out, and the best way to guard this trap door is to surround ourselves with committed people who will encourage us, support us, and refuse to accept any hint of non-commitment. Winners look for and play on winning teams. Commitment can be contagious!

10. Be a leader. Leaders turn losing teams into winning teams by injecting commitment into the members of the team. Bring commitment to others and you will have more for yourself, because commitment follows commitment around like a puppy dog, and multiplies when leaders give it the opportunity to do so.

CLOSING COMMENT

Like love and hate, success and failure are very closely related. Golfers win by one stroke. Football teams win by one point. Horses win by a nose. Competitive runners and swimmers win by microseconds.

Winners may only be inches ahead of their competition or their own past performance, but *they consistently look forward and move forward.* That's what makes them a success. In our own case, we may only need to be a tiny bit better than we already are to win.

As these examples have shown, to be truly productive, we need to be in an EXCITEMENT phase. We stay there by replacing our negative thoughts and feelings with positive action towards our dreams and goals.

The key to overcoming any fear we face is to maintain the original commitment clearly in front of us where it can help pull us forward. Since repeated negative cycles only serve to reduce our commitment with the downward spiral they produce, it is critical to repeat the positive cycle and strengthen our resolve instead.

Success is almost assured if we remain committed to our dreams, and we become Super Achievers when we learn to recommit on a regular basis over a long haul.

END OF CHAPTER SUMMARY

Failure IS an option – if you let it lead you to learning and course correction.

A high level of commitment gives you the edge you need to succeed.

You can *measure* your commitment.

You can *increase* your commitment by paying attention to these three variables:
> the payoffs
> the odds of success
> the amount of work required

Success in marketing, or any profession for that matter, is mostly a matter of recommitment, coupled with short-term action steps.

Recommitment is a choice – and a habit.

You can make the right split second choices, and doing so as a habit will lead you to success.

SPLIT SECOND CHOICE

Chapter 10

The Race: Get Up When You Fall

"Our greatest glory is not in never falling, but in rising every time we fall."

From the Chinese

"Fall seven times, stand up eight."

From the Japanese

"It's not how many times you get bucked off; it's how many times you get back on."

From the American Rodeo

"Perseverance is not a long race; it is many short races one after another."

Walter Elliott

THE RACE
(D. H. Groberg)

"QUIT! GIVE UP! YOU'RE BEATEN!" They shout out and plead,
There's just too much against you now, this time you can't succeed.
And as I start to hang my head in front of failure's face,
My downward fall is broken by the memory of a race.

And hope refills my weakened will as I recall that scene.
For just the thought of that short race rejuvenates my being.
A children's race, young boys, young men; now I remember well.
Excitement, sure, but also fear; it wasn't hard to tell.

They all lined up so full of hope. Each thought to win that race
Or tie for first, or if not that, at least take second place.
And fathers watched from off the side, each cheering for his son.
And each boy hoped to show his dad that he would be the one.

The whistle blew and off they went, young hearts and hopes of fire.
To win, to be the hero there, was each young boy's desire.
And one boy in particular, his dad was in the crowd,
Was running near the lead and thought, "My Dad will be so proud."

But as he speeded down the field across a shallow dip,
The little boy who thought to win, lost his step and slipped.
Trying hard to catch himself, his hands flew out to brace,
And mid the laughter of the crowd, he fell flat on his face.

So down he fell and with him hope. He couldn't win it now.
Embarrassed, sad, he only wished to disappear somehow.
But as he fell, his dad stood up and showed his anxious face.
Which to the boy so clearly said, "Get up and win that race!"

The Race: Get Up When You Fall

He quickly rose, no damage done — behind a bit, that's all,
And ran with all his mind and might to make up for his fall.
So anxious to restore himself to catch up and to win,
His mind went faster than his legs. He slipped and fell again.

He wished that he had quit before with only one disgrace.
I'm hopeless as a runner now, I shouldn't try to race.
But, in a laughing crowd he searched and found his father's face
That steady look that said again, "Get up and win the race."

So, he jumped up to try again. Ten yards behind the last.
If I'm to gain those yards, he thought, I've got to run real fast.
Exceeding everything he had, he regained eight or ten,
But trying so hard to catch the lead, he slipped and fell again.

Defeat! He lay there silently, a tear dropped from his eye.
There's no sense running anymore -- three strikes I'm out -- why try?
The will to rise had disappeared, all hope had fled away.
So far behind, so error prone, closer all the way.

I've lost, so what's the use, he thought, I'll live with my disgrace.
But then he thought about his dad, who soon he'd have to face.
"Get up," an echo sounded low. "Get up and take your place.
"You were not meant for failure here, get up and win the race."

With borrowed will, "Get up," it said, "You haven't lost at all.
"For winning is not more than this: to rise each time you fall."
So up he rose to win once more. And with a new commit,
He resolved that win or lose, at least he wouldn't quit.

SPLIT SECOND CHOICE

So far behind the others now, the most he'd ever been.
Still he gave it all he had and ran as though to win.
Three times he'd fallen stumbling, three times he'd rose again.
Too far behind to hope to win, he still ran to the end.

They cheered the winning runner as he crossed first place.
Head high and proud and happy; no falling, no disgrace.
But when the fallen youngster crossed the line, last place,
The crowd gave him the greater cheer for finishing the race.

And even though he came in last, with head bowed low, unproud;
You would have thought he won the race, to listen to the crowd.
And to his Dad he sadly said, "I didn't do so well."
"To me you won," his father said, "You rose each time you fell."

And when things seem dark and hard and difficult to face,
The memory of that little boy helps me in my race.
For all of life is like that race, with ups and downs and all,
And all you have to do to win is rise each time you fall.
"QUIT! GIVE UP! YOU'RE BEATEN!" they still shout in my face.
But another voice within me says, "GET UP AND WIN THE RACE!"

May God bless you and your family's future as you take
responsibility for your attitude.

Jim Winner

106

Epilogue

Near the end of the movie version of **Jonathan Livingston Seagull**, adapted from Richard Bach's magnificent book, Jonathan has a conversation with his student, Fletcher Lynd Seagull:

Jonathan Livingston Seagull:
  "It is time to return to the flock."
Fletcher Lynd Seagull:
  "Why?"
Jonathan Livingston Seagull:
  "You have a gift to give...
After pausing, Jonathan continues:
  "Vicious. Clumsy. A seagull hardly knows how to walk. But don't you see, Fletcher? A seagull wasn't made to walk. He was made to fly. And when he learns to fly, he's the purest, loveliest, most graceful creature alive. True for you. True for me. True for all the flock. We can soar free across the sky. But how often we don't want to. That's the gift we can give. To help those who want to learn find what they love to do."

This book was written for you — so that you, too, can fly above the clouds with a positive, productive attitude.

APPENDIX
SAMPLE COMMITMENT FORM

What am I committing to do as I begin this career (project, relationship, marriage)? What is my commitment?

_____

_____

_____

Why am I committed to this career (project, relationship, marriage)? What am I excited about? Who else is excited and why? What are my motives and reasons for undertaking this commitment?

_____

_____

_____

I would describe my dream of the future in the following way (include sights, sounds, smells, feelings):

_____

_____

_____

Fulfillment of this commitment will provide me with the following reward(s):

_____

_____

_____